DATA

SCIENCE

A Comprehensive Beginner's Guide to Learn the Realms of Data Science

William Vance

Table of Contents

Introduction

Data is a set of information that reflects values qualitatively or quantitatively. It can either be structured (properly categorized) or unstructured. Data science deals with all types of data. It is a multidisciplinary field that focuses on interpreting and orienting data using a scientific approach. It utilizes various scientific processes, algorithms, and systems. You may have come across terms like "big data" and "data mining." These have a similar concept to data science. While data mining deals more with just the process, data science deals with the analysis of the structure and function of the data. Data science involves using powerful hardware, good programming systems, and efficient algorithms. This guide gives you insights into the field of data science in a simplified and easy-to-understand manner.

Science can never be learned by isolating and segregating subjects. Newton could not have possibly put forth the theories related to Physics without knowing mathematics! Likewise, data science is developed using several arms of science, which include mathematics, statistics, computer science, and information science. Data science is a union of the concepts, techniques, and theories drawn from these different fields to understand the meaning of data. Rapid advancement in technology has had an immense impact on science. Jim Gray was a computer scientist who received the Turing award for his contributions to data science. He considered/ believed that data science is the fourth paradigm of science, the first three being empirical, theoretical, and computational. In 2015, the American Statistical Association identified database management, statistics, and machine learning, and distributed and parallel systems as the three emerging foundational professional communities.

Around the year 2008, companies worldwide realized that professionals specialized in handling, organizing, and analyzing considerably large sets of data have become necessary. That is when the term "data scientist" was coined. Google's chief economist, Hal Varian, acknowledged the importance of adapting to the upcoming technology and suggested reconfiguring existing systems in different industries.

An excellent data scientist can:

- Identify a relevant problem that needs to be solved;
- Collect information from various sources
- Organize the information systematically
- Analyze and interpret the data
- Generate results that answer the questions efficiently
- Share the result in a way that boosts the business

These skills have been deemed mandatory and beneficial for almost all industries. This has led to a higher recruitment of good data scientists. In the last decade, there has been an alacritous increase in the amount of data generated and retained by companies, as well as individuals (like you and me!). What to do with such massive amounts of data? Who would process and handle it? Who would see what statistics reflect? Someone must make meaning out of the piles of numbers and sets we have, right? That's what data scientists look after. Becoming a data scientist is sought after in recent years, so much that it has been titled as "the sexiest job of the 21st century" by Harvard University. Data scientists are so much in demand that McKinsey predicts that there will be a 50 percent gap in the supply of data scientists and their demand.

Don't you sometimes wish that the technology you see in the Hollywood sci-fi movies existed in real life? Well, this can actually happen by advancements in data science! Data science is the future of Artificial Intelligence. Therefore, it is very important to understand what data science is and how can it add value to your business.

Now, let's dig deeper into what data science is, its structure, and functioning!

Chapter 1

Data Science and the Data Scientist

Data is something that has no value if it is not processed correctly. The goal of data science is to uncover the meaning of the data. It is done by blending various tools, algorithms, and machine learning principles. The current decade had witnessed a swift magnification in all things related to computers and the Internet. Approximately 2.5 quintillion bytes of data is generated every day, which comes from various possible sources like:

Ø Sensors used in malls, offices, etc

Ø Digital media on our smartphones

Ø E-commerce transactions

Ø Social media posts

Data science deals with small data sets to really huge datasets (giving rise to "big data"). So, the traditional and the new approaches to analyzing these data differ slightly. The data generated these days fall into three categories: structured, semi-structured, and unstructured. According to the latest trends, it can be predicted that, at the end of 2020, more than 80% of the present data could be unstructured. How could we predict this, you ask? Data science is the answer!

Take a look at the picture below. It represents all domains where data science is making its mark and impacting it. It includes:

Ø Travel

Ø Marketing

Ø Healthcare

Ø Social media

Ø Sales and credit

Ø Insurance

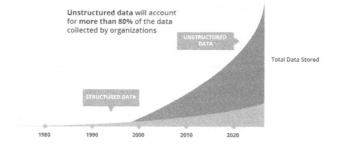

Consider data as the fuel and data science engine of the car of these industries. So the car runs because of the engine, which is, in turn, dependent on data. All of these domains work in a similar fashion.

Let's first look at where you do come across data science in your daily life:

• How easy is it to get a ride from Uber? Pretty simple, right? All you need to do is open the app, set your pickup and drop location, and book a cab. Then you conveniently get picked up and then pay with your phone or cash. Moreover, while booking the cab, you even get an estimate of when you will reach your destination, how much it will cost you, who's driving the cab, etc. Ever wondered how it is possible for these apps to show you all this information? The answer, again, is data science!

- Evolving techniques and scientific advancements can give significant predictions about the weather. The source for this information is satellites, ships, radars, etc. These also employ the use of data science. Using this, many a time, a possibility of a natural calamity can be predicted. This helps in saving a lot of lives.

- Have you ever wondered how you get all the purchase suggestions while surfing on the Internet? Doesn't it reflect the items similar to the ones you had looked upon the Internet recently? How does this work? All thanks to data science!

Data science utilizes a lot of skills like statistics, mathematics, and business domain knowledge. It helps organizations in:

Ø Reducing the costs

Ø Getting into new markets

Ø Appealing to various categories of the population

Ø Assessing the importance and need for certain campaigns

Ø Launching a new product or service

These are the various reasons why and how data science serves as an integral part of the culture and economy of the world:

1. A better understanding of customers

Data science works in a manner that is used to understand customers in a much-emancipated way. Customers are at the heart of any brand. So, they play a significant role in their profits or losses. Data science serves as an important link to connect brands with their customers in a personalized manner by understanding the precise requirements of customers. It involves understanding browsing history, purchase history, age, and income to recommend specific products required by the customer. Hence, data science ensures greater brand power and engagement with customers.

2. Connect to the audience

Data science helps brands to convey their story in a very engaging and comprehensive manner. They can inculcate every human emotion and thus can connect. This aids in better marketing of the brand. Customer feedbacks are analyzed to make decisions about a campaign. Therefore, it creates a better connection between the brand with the target audience.

3. Solve complications and make good decisions

By utilizing different tools and algorithms, big data helps other brands and organizations to answer major complications in various fields. They include IT, Human resources, and resources management effectively by using both materialistic and non-materialistic things. Many leading companies invest a considerable amount of money in data science to get the right information, and by using this information, they make the right decision.

4. **Relates to daily life**

Data science aids industries to make precise decisions and turns raw data into meaningful information. Some of these industries are major sectors, such as healthcare, finance, banks, business, start-ups, etc. These sectors are associated with people's daily lives, and hence, data science indirectly associated with the human community.

Statistics Vs. Data Science

Many people tend to confuse data science with plain statistics. Let's see how both these differ from each other.

The basic difference lies between explaining and predicting.

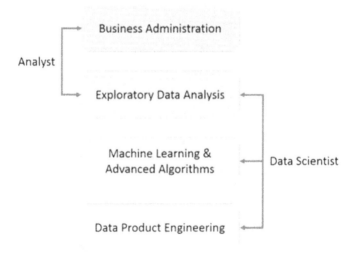

[Source - https://www.edureka.co]

8

A data analyst is responsible for explaining what the data represents. He processes the history of the data and describes the events occurring. Whereas, a data scientist is involved in an exploratory analysis of the data as well as identifying/predicting the occurrence of specific events by studying the patterns in the data using advanced tools. He/she has to consider the data with multiple points of view to make the most out of it.

Technically speaking, data science is used to make decisions and predictions using predictive causal analytics, prescriptive analytics, and machine learning. Let us understand these three things now.

- **Predictive causal analytics**

It is used to predict the likelihood of a particular event occurring in the future. Assume that you are providing financial aid on credit, then you need to make sure that your customers pay you back within a specific time frame. What usually happens is, predictive causal analytics is utilized in such scenarios, to understand the customer's payment patterns. It considers payment history and then calculates the possibility of future payments.

- **Prescriptive analytics**

This is an era of smart devices. With upcoming artificial intelligence, you'd even get to have a real "talk" with one of these apps/devices. So, it means we need to have algorithms to add "intelligence" in our devices to provide it with decision-making ability. To do so, data scientists use prescriptive analytics. Take, for example, Google's self-driving car. It cannot only make its own decisions but can also change it with dynamic parameters. Using complex algorithms, this car just knows when to turn, which path to take, when to go slow, or speed up!

- **Machine learning for making predictions**

Training machines is one more thing that data scientist deals with. Data science involves optimizing machine learning so that automated processes themselves can predict future trends. For example, transactional data of a finance company. This is categorized under supervised learning since the database for optimizing the machine is already present.

- **Machine learning for pattern discovery**

In case if you do not have the parameters for optimization of the data, then there is a need to find out the hidden patterns within the dataset. In contrast with the earlier section, this is an unsupervised model. Clustering is the most common algorithm used.

Responsibilities Of A Data Scientist

By now, it must've become clear to you that a data scientist is a professional who deals with various aspects of data science. A data scientist's way of working is like the why-why analysis. They will always ask why throughout the process. A data scientist needs to test different types of models and algorithms to check how they work. The point we're making is, they're curious about the data that is generated. They encompass the skills and functioning of a statistician, analyst, or engineer; data scientists perform little some of the tasks done by others. A data scientist needs to perform all that is specified by the company where he/she is working. But essentially the following are the methods that they need to perform:

1. Data analysis

2. Modelling/statistics

3. Engineering/prototyping

These are the core tasks that a data scientist usually performs in a similar order. One step before data analysis is data cleaning. This reflects the lifecycle of the data science process, which will be dealt with in further chapters.

Data Cleaning

As mentioned previously, there's a lot of data getting generated every day. Much of this data is in a format that is not readily useable. So, a data scientist's first job is to organize, format the data, and order it in a way that can be easily understood while following a set of specific rules.

Consider a CSV, which describes the finances of a fast food franchise containing information in multiple columns and rows. Say, for example, a company's IT department's employee names, language, qualifications, and the number of days leave are given in one sheet. This document is easy to read, understand, and process. Now, consider the same details present in different files in random order. The person processing these files now, should first gather the information and align it in a proper format. All unnecessary data should be ignored. Also, the person needs to make sure that the data entered makes sense. For instance, some columns might have "Master's in computer science" under the Name column while Robert Plant under the column "Education details." Data cleaning refers to aligning the data and fixing the errors. Once the data is properly assembled, further steps become easy and clear.

Data Analysis

A data scientist has to analyze a lot of data present in various excel sheets, as mentioned earlier. Here, he/she is responsible for plotting various graphs to understand it. It is a domain of visual results. Through data analysis, a data scientist tries to develop a story or put forward an easily understandable outcome. Sometimes, this task is simple (Like assessing what factors work best for onetime service users to turn into long-term clients). Sometimes, it can be time-consuming and difficult. One of the examples that will highlight what data analysis is: data scientists at Facebook assessed that having at least ten friends can ensure that a user stays online for long hours. So, it strives to help you connect to a lot more people and "make friends" on their site.

Modeling/Statistics

Depending on their background, a data scientist considers himself/herself as doing either modeling or statistics. In any of the cases, this is the step where theoretical knowledge of the data scientist becomes important. Once the data is assembled and understood, you need to predict something out of it. You need to make predictions from the given data or a similar dataset. In the earlier example of Facebook, the site tries to increase the number of friends. But how are they doing to do it? That answer would lie in this step, and the implementation will lie in the next. This is a very complex step. In this machine learning age, undoubtedly, you will get powerful algorithms with the potential to solve your problem. But it isn't easy to find the exact solution. A data scientist spends hours together, trying to evaluate and tweak the model to give out the best results.

Engineering/Prototyping

Merely having assembled and analyzed data, with a ready model isn't enough. What's the use of cooking food if there's nobody to eat it? Likewise, just having the models ready doesn't do anyone much good. What the data scientist needs to do now is to engineer and build a usable product out of it. Remember how I mentioned implementing the plan to increase Facebook friends? This is the step where they make these models available for the customers so that it can be used by commoners (people who are not data scientists). This can be in many forms: visual form (charts), a metric on the dashboard, or even an application. What a data scientist builds depends on the requirement/need, amount of data, and the final consumers.

Wrap Up

Remember how I mentioned that these processes reflect the life cycle? I am stressing on the word "cycle" more, so it has to come into a full circle. So, once everything is done, in the long run, with advancements in science and ever-changing demands/requirements, a data scientist has to go back to step 1. He/she has to go back to the analysis of the data that was created later to see how things are working or if they get another idea that can add value to the project. There can be countless reasons. The cycle keeps going on, and you find yourself up for a different challenge every time. That's the beauty of data science!

What role does a data scientist play in an organization?

1. Help the organization make good decisions

A data scientist finds its way into the core of the upper management team of a firm. He is trusted and is likely to be a primary advisor and a strategic partner of the organization. He/she is responsible for ensuring that the staff utilizes their analytics capabilities to the core. He/she communicated and exhibited the value of the organization's data to improve the decision-making stage. You will be responsible for various activities, including recording metrics, tracking of the data, etc. and other information listed down to you.

2. Defining goals and actions

A data scientist is required to examine and explore an institution's data. After a careful assessment, he needs to recommend and prescribe specific actions that would help to improve the organization's activity that engages more customers and eventually increase overall profitability.

3. Prioritize and maximize the efficiency

A data scientist needs to ensure that the staff of the organization is familiar and well-versed with the analytics product. They prepare the staff for adequate and proper use of the system so that meaningful insights can be extracted. He/she demonstrates the use and is responsible for making everyone understand it. Later, he/she also needs to understand the product capability. Only after that can he help the organization to shift the focus on addressing key business challenges.

4. Identifying opportunities

Identifying refers to the work, which is required to be completed as per the organization's current system. A data scientist must think deeply about the current system and believe in questioning the structure and the functioning of the same. He/she should be able to recheck the existing system and build his/her assumptions to develop some analytical algorithms. He/she may also think of some productive ways to make the current system efficient. Their main role lies in their analytical and structural thinking abilities, for which they get opportunities to improvise the organizational value derived from their data.

5. Testing vital decisions

While it comes to decisions, you should make sure that all your assumptions and theories are correct. Taking decisions can be very crucial while stepping on the next stone. You may always get confused about what and how to make a decision? What impact will the decisions have on the organization? In such a scenario, a data scientist has a vital role to play. He/she analyzes the previous

choice as a career path for young enthusiasts. It is often asked by an enthusiast, "What skills are required to become a data scientist?"

This part of the book will highlight the Technical and Non-Technical skills required to become a data scientist. After getting a skills overview, you would be motivated to start your career in data science.

Technical Skills

Some of the most critical/ important skill set is:

1. Knowledge about Probability and Statistics and how to apply them.

2. Knowledge about frameworks processes, mining data, and the current value of unstructured data.

You must mandatorily have good skills in mathematics, programming, and statistics. So, make sure you have an academic background relevant to the skills mentioned. Most of the data scientist has a higher level of educational qualifications. This creates a rigid base (with a technical point of view) to stay in the field of data science. Some schools and universities across the globe now offer courses and specialized programs exclusively to boost your data science career path.

For those who do not want to go for this approach, there are other options too. Online courses help you to know the gist behind practicing data science.

Other than having a strong background academically, you need to have the following technical skills.

Programming Skills

Having hands-on practice and thorough knowledge with some common programming languages is essential, with C++ being the oldest traditional language and Python being the trending but commonly used coding language. Programming languages help you in the steps of data cleaning and lets you adequately build a dataset that is unstructured.

Understanding of analytical tools

Analytical tools help you to extract the information of a dataset. There are different analytical tools you can go for. You can set up your skills in the utilization of these diagnostic instruments by getting different accreditations. Certifications of data science will be discussed in one of the later chapters to have an overview of the same.

Operating with unorganized information

Understanding unstructured data or information is one of the most crucial skills that is required to become a data scientist.

Non-Technical Skills

Non-technical skills include personal skills needed for succeeding in the field of data science. Only educational qualifications and certifications won't let you know if you're fit for being a data

scientist. Apart from educational qualifications, there are some special requirements for becoming a data scientist. Knowing what you're up for thoroughly is a lot deeper than that.

They are:

A business sense

All the technical skills that a data scientist has gained won't matter much if he doesn't have basic business acumen. How could you expect a data scientist to help and grow an organization's business if he doesn't understand business himself, right? So, to channel your abilities and to enable an association to perceive the issues and potential difficulties and issues, attempt and build up your essential marketing prudence.

Solid relational abilities

As an information researcher will undoubtedly know and comprehend the information superior to others in the organization. So, it is your job to deliver the information to others so that your organization can benefit from it. Thus, it turns into a need for you to have the option to convey the information to non-technical individuals effectively.

Great intuition at data

Data intuition skills can be gained only by experience. As you start handling datasets very often, you need to be able to intuitively perceive patterns and identify the exact position or nearness of the worth in the information bits. This way, you become more efficient and quicker in processing the data.

This chapter gave you a brief idea about what data science is and what the data scientists are. In the next chapter, you will understand the skills required for a data scientist in depth.

Chapter 2

Fundamentals of Data Science

In the previous chapter, we learned about what is data science and the need for data science. But the most common thing people think that learning some basics about data science is only required to excel in data science. Before diving in too deep, you must understand the fundamentals of data science. For this, you must know what is "data" what you are trying to do with the "data," and how will you apply any scientific principles, or how will you use tools to achieve your desired goals with that data?

What is data?
Data is a set of information required for further analysis.

What is the goal of data science?
The goal of data science is to use a particular tool to analyze and resolve the specific problem and give accurate results.

The Scientific Method
Scientific methods are the processes or algorithms used in data science.

Once you understand these three steps, then you are set to go deep into the process of data science.

Overview of Data Science

Data science is a trending technology that every company wants. Data science is an exciting field to become interested in. There is a large demand for talented, analytically minded people. All sized companies, whether they are small-sized enterprises, large-sized enterprises are hiring data scientists on a large scale. The data science role provides real-world, real value across a wide range of industrial applications. People generally approach this field by reading and researching sci-fi programs, which are generated by large research organizations. With the progressing technologies, data science is sub-categorized with various tools and algorithms. There is no stated definition of data science tools, and also data science is not limited to tools and algorithms such as Machine learning, deep learning, and NLP.

The commercial value of a data scientist is increasing day by day as they are responsible for providing clarity, results, and insights about the information, quantities that data can bring. This role can collate, collaborate, encompass everything from data engineering, to data analysis, classification to reporting with the addition of some algorithms like machine learning or deep learning. To conclude about the data scientist role, the skill sets required are broad and varied. In most of the companies, the Pareto rule or fabled rule of 80:20 is applied, where 80% of the value comes from 20% of the skill set.

Let's look at some fundamentals of data science that are required for an aspiring data scientist to master.

1. Start with Statistics

2. Assess your assumptions

3. Distribution > Location

4. Suitable Sampling

5. Data Engineering

6. Programming in Practice

7. Effective Coding

8. Communicate Clearly

9. The graphics game

Start with Statistics

The main attribute in which a data scientist contributes to his/her company is to make complex data and its computations in an easy and well sorted way. This can be achieved by understanding and utilizing statistics. What are statistics and the role of statistics in data science? Statistics lets you:

- Describe data, to provide a detailed overview to all stakeholders

- Comparing the data and hypotheses testing to provide information to businesses.

- Identify and compare old vs. new trends and establishing relationships that provide real-world predictive values from the data.

Statistical analysis is one of the powerful tools, which are used for commercial and operational purposes. The skill sets and detailing of statistical analysis and functions will be discussed in detail in one of the upcoming chapters. Thus, it is very vital to understand the fundamentals of statistical analysis for beginners. Various guiding principles help to understand such analysis in depth.

Assess your assumptions

Assessing your assumptions is one of the most important things. The result depends upon your assumptions. Always check the trends in your data before making any assumptions with the validity of your chosen stat test or methodology. Verify that your data meets all the underlying assumptions. If you miss any of these, you might end up making the wrong assumption. Many things depend upon your assumptions, such as whether your findings are interesting and are worth reporting.

It is important to know which approach you should not opt for rather than which approach you should take. As there are many ways to analyze your data or set of data, avoid common pitfalls. For example, in multiple comparisons scenario, you should not go for the same approach, which you used to generate it.

Distribution > Location

There is an established relationship between distribution and location. The distribution of a variable or data is usually as interesting or informative as its location.

The distribution of a variable is usually more interesting to understand as it contains information about the sampling processes. For example, the two types of data that follow have two distinct distribution patterns. The count data usually follows a Poisson distribution pattern, and the reinforcement system will follow a power-law distribution pattern. You should never depend on normally distributed data without manually checking it carefully. However, understanding the distribution of data is important for knowing how to deal with it! Most of the statistical methods rely upon your assumptions about how the data is distributed.

There are two distributions, namely unimodal and a bimodal distribution, which have the same mean, but they have different characteristics. If you disregard their distribution, you might lose crucial information.

An interesting example, which explains why it is necessary to check the data before reporting, take a look at Anscombe's quartet demonstrated below:

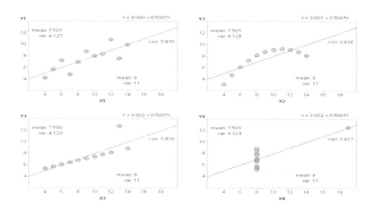

[Source - http://robslink.com]

These figures have different data; but nearly identical means, variances, and correlations. Each of the graphs looks very different but has identical summary statistics.

The certainty of the true value is revealed from the distribution of a variable distribution. For getting higher certainty, the distribution is "narrow," whereas, for less certainty, the distribution is usually "wide."

Suitable sampling

Suitable sampling means you have to choose the best-suited sampling process for your project. Every sampling must be carefully implemented to produce high-end results. For illustration purposes, we can check a few testing methods like A/B testing, Bayesian Methods, etc. A/B testing is a test that explains how the products and platform can be optimized at a base level without having to cause a significant disturbance to businesses. A/B testing is an industry-standard used for comparing different versions of products. Whereas, the Bayesian method works well with smaller data sets if you have informative sets of prior data to work from. Every data collection has some limitations. You must be able to identify or recognize them.

Survey data can be sampling biased, where respondents who have the strongest opinions take more time to complete any survey. The below figure illustrates A/B testing:

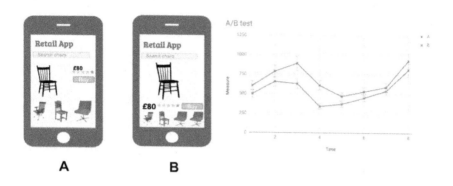

A   B

[source - https://cdn-media-1.freecodecamp.org]

Time and data can be affected by autocorrelation. And lastly, check for multicollinearity while analyzing data from any related sources.

Data Engineering

While working on a project, data engineering is important as most of the time, sourcing, cleaning, and storing new raw data in the data workflow for having more upstream analysis is preferred rather than actually implementing statistical tools and algorithms from scratch. Most of the statistical tools have inbuilt workings wrapped up in R packages and coding modules, i.e., Python modules.

Data Engineering also includes the "extract-transform-load" (ETL) process, which is a key process for the success of any data science team and is followed by most large companies. Larger companies, including all MNC, will have dedicated data engineers to implement this process to evaluate complex data infrastructure requirements. Whereas, small-scale companies and start-ups prefer data scientist to perform all-around data engineering and possess strong skills similar to a data engineer.

Programming in practice

A programmer must have high analytical skills as well as domain-specific knowledge with solid programming skills. To become a data scientist, you may wonder which programming languages are to be learned. There are many programming languages; not all can be learned at once, and there is no specific language that you have to learn. But most of them prefer the programming language of Python or R.

Both languages will help you to kickstart your programming journey. They make the best starting point if you work with data and datasets. Whichever language you prefer, you should aim to become familiar with all its structure, coding, features, and surrounding ecosystem. After selection of any particular language, you must browse various modules and packages available, get familiar with the API's which you may require for accessing your company's core platform and services.

Knowing about databases is also equally important. You may start with the SQL server database, and then you may want to switch to other databases. NoSQL databases are also worth learning database; you can go for this database if your company uses it.

Start with simple scripting, and repetitive tasks, including the same scripting, will boost you, and you will become confident. Writing long scripts may be difficult initially, but once you are confident about the scripting and get familiar with the scripts, you can boost yourself to go behind long interesting scripts. This way, you will learn to program in a few months.

Effective Coding

Once you are familiar with writing programming scripts/codes, it is of utmost importance to have a check on what you have written. Initially, a code debugger act as a helping assistant. But as you move on to higher and bigger scripts, you should be sure that you have written the code effectively. Reusability plays a vital role in effective coding. It is worth to invest some of your hours in writing codes at an abstraction level, which will, by default, enable it to be used more than once. However, there should be a proper balance between short and long-term priorities. For example, any code, which is not reusable, do not invest your time in practicing the same. There are management tools that streamline the deployment and maintenance of the code. It is also possible to automate your routine processes with the help of task schedulers. To ease your work, you can make use of regular code reviews and look upon the standard documentation. Also, you can make use of certain frameworks such as Airflow, which helps in scheduling and monitoring ETL processes making them easier and more robust. Apache Spark and Hadoop are beneficial for distributed data storage, and it's processing. For a beginner, it is not advised to go in such depth, but knowing about this is an advantage.

Effective Reporting

Effective reporting forms the base of data science communication. To bring up the commercial value of any organization, you must have effective communication. There are four primary aspects of effective reporting:

- **Accuracy**

In this step, you will know how to interpret your results while evaluating any limitations and loopholes that may apply. Hence, this is a crucial step. Accuracy while interpreting and collecting is important to help avoid pitfalls. One should avoid over or understating any particular result.

- **Precision**

Further to accuracy, precision also matters because any ambiguity in your report may have a negative impact, as well as it would misinterpret the findings. It will affect every result down the line.

- **Concise**

Always have a habit of preparing and keeping your report shortly. But make sure it doesn't become too shorter. Longer reports are not advised and not appreciated at higher levels. A good format will have the context of the main question, a brief description of the data, and give an overview of results and graphics in the form of a headline. If you have any extra information to be included, keep it an appendix. Avoid mixing up the main information with less important information.

The Graphics Game

The graphics game or graphical representation is always at the top of the data pyramid. It includes data visualization, which will help you to interpret as well as communicate complex results to stakeholders. The graphical representation is much more effective than paragraphs of text when you are required to explain some information to the stakeholders.

We had listed a few free as well as paid visualization and dashboard building tools like Plotly, Tableau, Chartio, etc. And many more.

You can also opt for modern tools like Microsoft Excel spreadsheets or Google Sheets. But these sheets lack specific functionalities that a purpose-built visualization software has. Also, some guiding principles are specially designed to build dashboards and graphics; you can make use of such principles.

The major challenge is to maximize the visualization of the information value without compromising "readability."

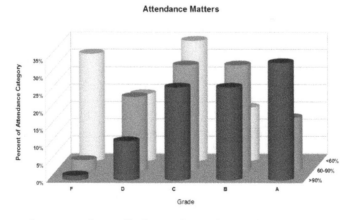

[source - https://cdn-media-1.freecodecamp.org]

Consider a graphical representation of Attendance where on the X-axis "Percent of Attendance" is mapped whereas on the Y-axis, "Grade" is mapped. This graphical representation is interesting to watch, yet difficult to understand at first glance. You must always keep your representation simple rather such complex representation. Make your graphics as simple as you can with most of the information; this way, you will be able to display more information with lesser time. Complex graphics consumes more time to be explained as well as it takes greater time for stakeholders to understand and digest the same information.

Finally, the skills required for great data visualization are associated with UX and graphical design. You must be familiar with all these to become aware of data visualization and how it works. Data science requires a diverse skill set. This four core skills listed below highlights a great value to kickstart your journey with data science:

Statistical analysis, including the base theory as well as real-world applications.

Ø Programming/Coding in at least one programming languages i.e., Python or R as well as databases like SQL and NoSQL.

Ø Best practices of data Engineering

Ø Communicating your work effectively.

Now let us take a look at some broad methods and theories.

Probability and Statistics

Probabilities and Statistics form the base of methods and theories in data science. In probability, any given precondition of the dataset can result in a specific way. There are certain techniques and methods that you must be familiar with for applying probability and statistics in data science. The major techniques can be listed as "Probability Distributions," "Statistical Distribution," Two characteristics of data," and "Common Probability Distributions." Some more methods, maybe "Baye's Rules," "Bayesian Inference," and Joint and Conditional Probabilities."

Decision Theories

Decision-making is one of the most important fundamentals of data science. Whether the decision theory is applied in engineering or business fields, we will always try to make decisions using data. Imagine a scenario where you have the data in front of you, but is it trying to tell you something? If no, then that's only data. But if it's telling you something, that means you are manipulating it by making some decisions and knowing exactly what the data is trying to tell us. But have you ever thought about how the data makes us make decisions? What are those factors, which go into the decision-making process? What are the different methods to make appropriate decisions? The Normal Hypothesis and Binary Hypothesis Tests are the starter tests required for excelling in data science. There are many more like Bayes Risk, Optimal Decision-Making strategies, which are beneficial.

Estimation Theory

After you make a decision, estimate the results, which is the immediate next step of Decision theory. Sometimes you have to estimate certain characteristics of the data, which may include averages, certain parameters, etc. The main estimation theories you may refer to are "Unbiased Estimation," "Kalmar Filter," and "Likelihood Estimation."

Coordinate Systems

The coordinate system refers to aligning the data from various data elements into a common framework. It is strongly recommended to gain knowledge of coordinate systems and how they are used. There are many books you can refer to for information about coordinate systems, some of the books are "Euclidian spaces," "Cartesian coordinate system," "Spherical coordinate system," and "Polar Coordinate system." You can Google a few more books on the coordinate systems and learn its properties.

Linear Transformations

Linear Transformation is one of the basic steps taken after having the idea of coordinate systems. Once you get familiar with coordinate systems, the linear transformation may become easier to understand. By this step, you can learn how the data is transformed and why to transform the data to get underlying information. Transformations like "Matrix Multiplication," "Fourier Transforms," "Uncertainty Principle," and " Wavelet Transforms" help to transform data into other data products through various transformations. There are multiple reference books available in the market for basic enlightenment on all types of transformations.

Computational Effects of Data and Dataset

When we hear the term "computation", we think of complexity. Computations are represented in various forms; one of the most common forms is the Mathematical Representation of Computation. The others may be listed as Reversible Computation, Irreversible Computations, etc. There is always an impact on the information when you are applying algorithms or computations on the data. The result may be affected by the algorithms and computations if they are not applied correctly, resulting in a negative effect on the result.

Prototype Coding / Programming

As we have already learned how important programming is for taking a step towards data scientists. You should be able to write programs that access the particular data, process the data as per the methods, and visualize the data in important languages. Some common types of programming languages are C, C++, C#, Python, R, etc. Some of the databases are SQL, NoSQL, etc. Familiarity with functions and variables is recommended.

Theory of Graph

Graphs are responsible for connecting information between different data elements. The commonly practiced graphs are "Undirected graphs," and "Directed graphs." You should refer to basic theory books like "Introduction to Graph Theory," "Graphical

Analysis," which may boost your confidence while working on graphs.

Algorithms

Data science is incomplete without algorithms. You must be able to understand the algorithms, and you are set to apply some. From where you will start? Start with basic algorithms like Recursive Algorithms, Heuristic Algorithms, Randomized Algorithms, Greedy Algorithms, and Shortest Path Algorithms. Then you can jump to some complex algorithms like series, parallel, and distributed algorithms.

Machine Learning

No wonder that Machine Learning is the most important and crucial phase of data science. It tops the list of the fundamental of data science. Machine learning is used at a larger scale than any other tool or programming language. We have a separate chapter for Machine learning to learn in-depth. Some of the main things you should understand in Machine learning are Decision tree structures, Hidden Markov models, Basic linear classifiers, Neural networks by Deep learning, Clustering, and Vector quantization.

Chapter 3

Understanding the Life Cycle
and Art of Data Science

Data Science Process

Data science is widely used in the context of an organization. When you are being asked to perform a data science-based project, the foremost step you will take will be preparing a project charter. Charter, in usual terms, means "Agenda." Whenever you organize any meeting, you will prepare an agenda, without which the meeting would have no definition. Similarly, a project charter is prepared as the initial step, which contains every detail, such as your research data, how your project will benefit your organization, schedule, data you will be needing, type of resource, and lastly, deliverables.

After this step comes to the second step: Retrieving data - In the first step, you've already mentioned about the data and resources you would be wanting. You must ensure that you should be able to use the data in your program. By this, you are checking the existence of quality and access to the data. Some data can be also be delivered by third-party companies in the form of excel or different types of open source databases.

The next step can be considered the most important and crucial step:

Data Collection - Data collection is always performed in subsequent steps. This is the step where you may commit mistakes more often. Hence, it is known as the most crucial step. The data collection process is subdivided into three phases - data cleaning, data integration, and data transformation.

- **Data cleaning** - It helps to remove any false or error values from the data sources and irregularities, instabilities, and inconsistencies from the data sources.

- **Data Integration** - Integration is a process of combining anything; it may be information or any other thing. Similarly, in this step, data integration plays a vital role in integrating information from various data sources and then combining them to get enriched data.

- **Data Transformation** - This step helps in transforming your data in a suitable format, which you can use for the program.

Following the data collection process comes an exploration of data:

Data Exploration – data exploration is responsible for developing a deeper understanding of your data. For example, how your variables work with each, how the data is being distributed, and whether the data is an outlier or not. This can be understood by some statistics or visual techniques and simple modeling. This step is usually abbreviated as EDA, i.e., Exploratory Data Analysis. Once this step is understood, you can process data Modeling.

Data Modeling Process - As the name suggests, the use of models, domain knowledge is required to analyze the insights about the data, which you got from all the previous steps. There are many processes set for data science; you can go for any process, i.e., Statistics, machine learning, operational research technique, etc. Building a data model is a mathematical process that involves selecting, executing, and diagnosing the variables of the model.

Life cycle

The life cycle of data science is divided into main 6 phases. Let us look at each step in detail:

Step 1 - Discovery - While selecting your project, there must be regular checkpoints before proceeding further. You must understand the various specifications, what is the requirement, what is to be prioritized, and the budget amount, which would be required for the project. If you have any dubiety, you must ask the right questions to the right stakeholders. You must also have a check on resources present in terms of physical resources, technology, time, and data for the project. Lastly, you will have to frame business problems. And formulate the analysis.

Step 2- data Preparation - In this phase, you can go for an analytical sandbox or shark tank approach to perform analytics, useful for the overall duration of the project. Analytical Sandbox is a standard process followed by most of the professionals. Shark tank is the process used mostly in the corporate world. Firstly, you have to prepare the sandbox structure, after preparing the sandbox, to get your data into the sandbox, you will have to perform a test known as ETLT (extract, transform, load, and transform). Before you perform data modeling, you will need to explore, pre-process, and condition your data properly. As described in the process of data science above, data cleaning, data integration, and data transformation can be performed by using the R method. This will eventually help you to stop the outliers. Once the data is cleaned and prepared, you can do the exploratory analytics.

Step 3 - Model Planning - In this phase, you will think of planning the methods and techniques to establish relationships between various variables and datasets. These relationships would act as a base point for all the algorithms, which you will implement in the latter stage. There are three common tools for model planning tools viz. R, SQL Analysis Services, and SAS/ACCESS.

To this stage, you have entered into your data and have decided which algorithms are to be used. Later, to this stage, you will be applying an algorithm and building the model.

Step 4 - Model Building - This phase is exclusively for training and testing of the datasets. You will examine your existing tools for efficiency and if they are appropriate for running the current models. You must also look for a robust environment while performing processing. Analyzing various basic techniques like classification, association, collection, and clustering are required while building a data model. The most common but popular tools for model building are depicted below:

- SAS Enterprise

- WEKA

- SPCS Modeler

- MATLAB

- Alpine Miner

- Statistica

Step 5— Operationalize: In this phase, you will be responsible for documenting all the required data, including final reports, briefings, codes, and any technical documents, if any. As this an operational phase, it is a must that you operationalize the documents in a proper manner. There are some autopilot projects as well, which are implemented in a real-time environment. You will get a complete overview of the performance and other irregularities before your project deployment.

Step 6 - Communicate Results: This is the last but most important phase of the life cycle, where you will actually analyze the work you have done so far. So how will you do this? You must try to evaluate whether you are successful in achieving the desired goal or it is a failure, and you need to work on it again. You will identify all the major findings from your project and communicate with stakeholders to understand their views on the same. They will analyze your work based on their criteria, if they are satisfied with your work, then you have completed the project. If they are not satisfied with your work, you are supposed to refine your work, or sometimes you will have to redefine the work and start it from the initial step.

Data Science as an Art

Data science is the science of data, analyzing the data. Data Analysis is not as easy as it looks. The data science process can be explained in detail by very few people. People do take efforts in analyzing data on a daily basis with either of the techniques, but most of them fail in their efforts because the professionals in data analysis have neither explained how data is analyzed nor shared their experience while doing so. This is the reason we call data science an "art." Art can be very much related to data analysis. Data science cannot be called as a concept, which is usually used to teach a computer about their techniques. But it is a form of art like data analysts use different tools to get their work done; then, it may range from linear graphs or linear regressions to various classifications. It is said the computer knows better than us; similarly, all these tools are well known to the computer. But the computer is not intelligent enough to track the correct tool and resolve the problem. In such a case, data analysts come into the picture where they actually figure out the perfect way in which the problem may be resolved, and accordingly, they gather and make use of the tools, integrate them into the data to develop the correct answer to the problem.

However, there is no proper documentation of the process of data analysis to date. You can read a number of books written on statistics and probability, but they lack to address the real-world data analysis solution. There are also many important frameworks established, which include classifying elements of data analysis using complex language. Mathematics can be one language. Complexing analysis can be achieved by this analysis, which produces accurate results as well.

The analysis cycle follows a linear, step-by-step process that has advanced level results. However, data analysis is a nonlinear approach that is embedded in various epicycles. In this approach, the information, which you have used, is checked at each step, which then decides the step is required to be undone, or it can proceed towards the next step. Certain analyses might be fixed and linear due to algorithms, which are encapsulated in the different software.

Usually, a study of data includes the creation and implementation of a plan for collecting and gathering data, whereas analysis means the data is already gathered. The data analysis study will be involving the fundamentals like hypothesis creation, data collection procedure design, collecting data from various resources, and interpretation of the data.

There are Five Major Activities of Data Analysis:

- State and refine the question

- Explore the data

- Create formal statistical models

- Interpret the results

- Communicate the results

For all the above activities, you must include the following steps:

1. Define or set the expectations

2. Collect information

3. Compare the data to your expectations

If the data doesn't match with your desired/expected results, you have to redo or fix the data so that the data you have a match with your expectations. Performing the above three steps is known as the cycle of data analysis. Every step will give you a new challenge while stepping forward towards the next step. It may happen that you will have to redo, undo, fix the data multiple times while you navigate through every step of the analysis, you will go through the epicycle to rigorously revise your documentation viz. Questions, basic or formal models, interpretation, and communication. The repeated cycle through each of the above five major activities constitutes the largest part of data analysis.

Define the Expectations

In this step, you define the expectations while laying down what you expect before you can perform anything such as planning a procedure, inspection of your data, or typing of a command. For professional data analysts, creating expectations is as easy as oiling any vehicle engine. For beginners, it is not an impossibly tough job to learn. But you have to do a thorough study of this to exempt in defining and creating expectations. For example, if you are visiting any shopping malls with your friends with no cash in hand, but you want to withdraw cash from ATM. Then you have to think and decide on what the minimum amount of money would be sufficient. You must have some expectations of the price in your mind before planning to withdraw the money. This exemplifies that you have prior knowledge of the price you need to withdraw. Another example of prior knowledge can be: When you are visiting a restaurant in the late evening or night, you must know what the closing time of the restaurant is. Using this information, you can plan your visit to that restaurant within time. If you don't have any idea of the closing time, you can always opt for Googling the time to know the exact working hours of the restaurant. All these things are very basic, but equally important. Such procedures that you apply to get prior information are useful to develop expectations. This procedure is similar in every main activity of the analysis process while implementing an analysis procedure.

Information Collection

In the information collection step, you will collect information related to the mentioned question or data. For the data, by using the above prior knowledge procedure or if you developed the expectations about the results, it is advised to carry out the operation once the data is inspected. The outcome of this activity may be the data that you need to collect and determine whether the collected data is as per your desired expectations.

Comparison of Expectations

Once you have the data readily available with you, the next step would be comparing the data with your expectations. By comparison, you would probably end up with these two possible results:

1. Your expectations are matching accurately with the data

2. Your expectations are not matching, and hence it has failed.

For example, consider you are about to match your cost estimations and final amount. If both the entities match accurately, then you can move to the next step. But in the event, if the cost estimation and the final amount doesn't match like if your expectations cost $50, but the check is $25, then you have failed to match. There might be two possibilities of getting different amounts in the latter example. First, you may have made the wrong expectations, and you need to revisit and correct it. Secondly, is the wrong check, possibly containing errors and irregularities.

Machine Learning

Machine learning refers to learning techniques for the systems from various types of data that they process. It is much easier to train a system on particular data to predict decisions. The training process is continuously allowing the system to predict, update, and make decisions. Some systems, like Gmail, Outlook, etc. Use spam filters, which are great examples of applied machine learning systems. Such systems use Bayesian filters to take and change decisions. These predictions and decisions help such a system to remain one step ahead of the spammers. Another example can be credit approvals, which use neural-networks that use machine learning techniques. Data scientists have always preferred using Machine-learning techniques as the first method while evaluating any data. That is the reason why machine learning is known as game-changer. What makes Machine learning of so much importance? There are four characteristics of Machine intelligence:

1. It is based on a strong foundation of a theoretical breakthrough

2. It redefines the current economic paradigm

3. The final result is commoditization

4. It unearths/reveals new data from data science

Supervised and Unsupervised Learning

Machine learning can be subdivided into two broad categories: Supervised and Unsupervised learning.

Supervised Learning – In this type of learning, the system makes decisions depending on the type of data entered. For example, you can say automated credit card approvals and spam filters on the mails follow the supervised learning technique.

When the system is supplied with a past/historical data samples of inputs and outputs, it establishes the relationship between the data using supervised learning.

Unsupervised Learning – In this type of learning, the system makes decisions depending upon only the input data without a corresponding output variable. Unsupervised learning builds a model of the underlying structure of the data so that you can be able to learn more about the data. It is known as "unsupervised" because it is not supervised by the total data, and the resulting data may or may not be inaccurate. Examples of unsupervised learning can be cluster analysis. In cluster analysis, you have to select a group of entities, which has different attributes, and divide them and categorize these entity spaces based on how far or near they are. Another example can be factor analysis, i.e., predictions and forecasting data. But they both differ in terms of outcome, which they produce. Predictions are focused on highlighting a single outcome, whereas forecasts have multiple outcomes in the form of probabilities.

Chapter 4

Overview of the Data Science Technique, Modeling and Featurization

To start your career as a data scientist, you need to be an expert in mathematical and statistical analytics, and also you should be well-versed in coding. The coding skills form a major part of data science. You must be able to play with data and dataset with ease. You must be an expert in one of the particular subject matter. Unless you are an expert in a particular subject, you are just a mathematician or statistician. To illustrate, a person without having knowledge or expertise in software tools and its analytics may be a software programmer and is called a software engineer or a developer, but not a data scientist.

As the demand for data insights have increased enormously, every organization is willing to adopt data science. There are experts in every discipline who are using data science under certain titles that can be listed as ad-tech data scientist, director of banking data scientist/analyst, geoengineer data analyst, clinical data scientist, geospatial analytics data analyst/scientist, political analyst, retails customization data scientist, and clinical informatics analyst in pharmaceutics. Let us now have a broader look at the key components that are part of a data scientist role:

Collecting, Querying and Consuming Data

Commonly, a data engineer's role is to capture and collate large volumes of structured, unstructured, and semi-structured data. Sometimes, like while processing the data, the normal capacity of the conventional database is exceeded, as it doesn't fit into the structural requirements of the traditional database architecture. Again, the task of a data engineer is a way to different but easier than a data scientist. Data scientists are more focused on the analysis of the data, predicting the results, and visualization of the data. But there is some similarity in the functionality of data science with a data engineer in terms of data collection, querying, and consuming the data during the analysis process.

Though it is said that valuable insights can be generated from a single source of data or datasets, the combination of multiple but relevant sources tends to deliver more contextual information that results in better data-informed decisions. The advantage that a data scientist has is that they are able to work from several datasets which they combine to get enough information that is stored in a single database, or they can be in from different databases. Often, the source data is stored and processed on a cloud-based platform. This cloud-based platform is built by software or by data engineers.

If you are a data scientist, you have no choice than querying data, i.e., Writing commands or programs to get relevant datasets from any data source. This is valid for a single database data source or combined database. In simple terms, most of the time, you will use Structured Query Language (SQL) to query data. When you are working with an application or doing any custom analyses using any programming language such as R or Python, you may choose any universally accepted file formats, which are listed below:

➢ Comma-Separated Values (CSV) Files:

It is common and the universally accepted file format. Almost every large-scale company and web-based analysis application accepts this type of file. It also accepted by many of the commonly used scripting languages such as Python and R.

➢ Scripts:

Almost all data scientists know about scripting languages like Python or R programming, which they use to analyze and visualize the data. These script files have extension .py or. ipynb (Python) or. R (R).

➢ Application Files:

One of the examples of the application files can be a commonly used Excel sheet. It is useful for analysis applications such as ArcGIS and QGIS, which have their proprietary file formats (the .MDX extension for ArcGIS and the .qgs extension for QGIS).

➢ Web Programming Files:

If you are trying to build customized, web-based data visualization, you may use data-Driven Documents to work with. This is a JavaScript library specially designed for data visualization purposes. When you need to work with D3.js, you can use that data to manipulate the web-based documents using hypertext Markup Language (HTML), SVG, and .css files.

Data Science Techniques Overview

When we say techniques, it includes everything related to analyzing, gathering, conceptualization, and contextualizing data. If you are thinking deeply about becoming a data scientist, you would probably enjoy working with all the new emerging technologies. With the development of Machine Learning and the latest technology of Deep Learning, which has worked with neural networks, it's interesting to jump in with such technologies. These technologies are proving very beneficial to researchers. Data scientists continue to enjoy these innovations and new technologies. You can say a data scientist is an all-rounder who has strong knowledge about statistics, coding, and software engineering tools. In short, a data scientist must have a mixture of skills viz. Scripting, coding, critical thinking, and statistical ability. You must excel in your skills in statistics as well as programming. A data scientist should understand all the basics and would be able to make a map out of a dot. For example, he must understand the ideas behind different techniques so that they understand how and when to use that method. It is obvious that you must get acquainted with simpler methods first to understand the complex ones. Also, you must know how to check the efficiency of your work. The more efficient your work is, the more accurate the results you get. Data science is an interesting field for researching purposes that has significant applications in many industries like science, finance, medical, etc., to name a few. But statistics is a major component, which must be known by any data scientist. We are introducing some statistical learning problems below, which may be useful for learning statistics.

Examples of Statistical Learning problems include:

➤ Personalizing an email spam detection system.

➤ Finding out the possibility of having a heart attack of a person by analyzing clinical measurements, demographic data, and diet.

➤ Classification of tissue samples into different cancer families.

➤ Identification of the relationship between demographic variables and attendance of the population survey.

Before jumping into the data science techniques for effectively dealing with larger datasets, it is recommended to understand the difference between statistical learning and Machine learning. We have a separate chapter for statistical analysis and tools as well as for Machine learning. You will get a brief description of both the processes in the upcoming chapters.

The difference can be:

1. Statistical learning started as a branch of Statistics.

2. Machine Learning started as a branch of Artificial Intelligence (AI).

3. Statistical learning concerns models and their interpretability, uncertainty, and precision.

4. Machine Learning includes all this and also it has an advantage in a Marketing firm.

1. Linear Regression

Linear Regression refers to the prediction of a target in terms of statistics. Linear regression prediction of a target is achieved by having the right linear relationship between the dependent and independent variables or data. The perfect result is achieved when there is a small deviation in the sum of all distances between the shape and previous observations. This is the best fit, as there will be no other position that can have such a small error. Linear Regression is again sub-divided into two broad types:

Ø Simple Linear Regression

Ø Multiple Linear Regression

In simple linear regression, you will have a single independent variable/data, which predicts a dependent variable/data by having the finest linear relationship. Whereas, multiple regression refers to having multiple independent variables/data to predict a dependent variable/data.

2. Classification

Classification is a data mining technique. This technique is a type of analysis that is used to assign features to a set of data to get an accurate analysis as well as predictions. There are two types of classification techniques commonly used for the analysis of an advanced data set:

1. Logistic Regression

2. Discriminant Analysis

Logistic Regression

As the name suggests, this is a logistic regression in which the analysis is performed when you have a binary variable, but it must be a dependent variable. It is best used to describe data and explain the association between one dependent binary variable and a nominal dependent variable.

Discriminant Analysis

In Discriminant Analysis, the data clusters are commonly known a priori. Based on the data, any new observation is classified as per population based on the types of features that are to be measured. This method is used for the distribution of 'A' independent predictors in each and every response class. Depending upon the nature of the models, they can be distinguished between the linear model or quadratic model.

Quadratic Discriminant Analysis.

Quadratic Discriminant Analysis is an alternative choice for the previous method. By this method, it is assumed that the observations or predictions are drawn from a class of 'B' and come from the Gaussian Distribution. The covariance matrix may be the other assumption made in this type.

Linear Discriminant Analysis

We have come across the observations and predictions of the data by discriminant analysis, but how is the discriminant scores are calculated? The answer to this query is "Linear Discriminant Analysis." By this technique, you will able to measure the "discriminant scores" for each of the observations you perform, which are detected by the linear combinations of independent variables. In this method, there is an assumption that all the observations recorded in each dataset come from Gaussian distribution.

3. Subset Selection

This method is used for searching for a subset of 'x' predictors that can be related to the response. Further, a model is built by selecting the least number of squares of the same subset features.

The Best Subset Selection

In this type of selection, a different regression i.e., Ordinary Least Square (OLS), is selected and applied for each possible combination of 'x' predictors and to the observation of the model to fit it. The algorithm used in this selection generally has two stages:

1. You should fit a model with 'k' predictors.

2. Highlighting of cross-validated prediction.

Here also, one should be careful and should not forget to use the validation error. This is because RSS and R2 may increase monotonically with the variable increase. How will you cross-validate? The best way would be to use the highest R2 while having the lowest RSS value to estimate the error.

Forward Stepwise Selection

Forward Stepwise Selection works in a straight manner where smaller subsets of x predictors is considered, and is initiated without a predictor model. Predictors are added to the model until the model is packed with all the predictors.

Backward Stepwise Selection

Backward Stepwise Selection works exactly in the opposite manner. Here, the model is packed with predictors all the time. The lowest predictor is removed from the model each time.

4. Shrinkage

Shrinkage is best used for the model having all the predictors packed in itself. Here, Backward stepwise selection is utilized. The estimated coefficients are thrown out each time from the model and made to zero, which depends on the least square estimates. Mostly, the backward selection is used, but other methods are also approached; in the even, any other method is used, the coefficients can be neared to approximate zero. Shrinking has two major techniques listed in the books, viz. Ridge Regression and Lasso.

Ridge Regression

Ridge Regression is somewhat similar to the least-squares analysis having the only difference in the estimation of the coefficients. By this step, RSS is reduced when you tend to select a coefficient using Ridge Regression. Also, a notable feature is that there is a penalty when the coefficients approach zero. This penalty, by all means, affects the estimates of the coefficient to near the zero. Hence, while applying ridge regression, it is important that you remove all the traits, even any of the smallest column space variance. The main issue with Ridge Regression is that you will have all the x predictors available in the final model too. Hence or otherwise, the penalty sets all the predictors back to zero. Usually, this doesn't make it impossible to estimate the result; still, you can even predict accurately. The only drawback is that it becomes a little difficult to interpret the final results.

Lasso

Lasso works a similar way as the ridge regression, but the only difference is that it forces the specific coefficients to near the zero as long as it has a smaller value. Lasso can rectify the problem, which usually happens in Ridge Regression.

5. Dimension Reduction

Dimension Reduction helps to reduce the issue of approximation of the X+1 coefficient to a simpler problem, i.e., N+1 coefficient (N<X). This can be achieved through the use of a computing technique. Here, you have to compute N different linear combinations and variable projections. Here, N projections are being extracted and are used as predictors in the linear regression model.

Principal Components Regression

The extraction of a low-dimensional set of properties from a vast/big group of variables is what principal components Regression is all about. The initial principal component value of the data has the observations, which change a lot. This usually means that the initial component represents a straight line that fits the data closely. You can fit x distinct principal components. The very next principal component follows the linear combination of variables steps that are different from the initial principal component, and it contains the highest variance that is subjected to the constraint. Using linear combinations in orthogonal directions, the principal component retains the variance in the original data. Principal Component Regression method includes highlighting the linear combinations of P that would represent the best P predictors. This method follows the unsupervised learning technique as P predictors are dependent on the response of Q in determining the principal component directions. In other terms, Q is unable to supervise the selection of any of the principal components. It is not guaranteed that whatever the directions are used to define the predictors can be used for the prediction of response. Partial least square can be an alternative to supervised learning; it works differently. It selects new smaller sets of features embedded with a linear combination of previous features. It is used to highlight the response of the new features.

6. Nonlinear Models

In this type, the observation of the data is modeled by the use of a nonlinear combination function of the parameters. It is dependent on more than one, or you can say multiple but independent variables. Data is mostly applied by the successive approximation technique. There are a few nonlinear model techniques, which you must be familiar:

A Piecewise Function

This is a common function wherein its function is to apply a specific interval to the main domain's function by the help of multiple sub-functions. In this type of function, you can express the function instead of the characteristic function itself.

A Spline

When you perform a piecewise function with the use of a polynomial, then it is known as a spline function. In computer language, the graphic representation is performed using this function. It represents a piecewise polynomial parametric curves. It represents a popular curve as a result of simplicity in the construction.

7. The Tree-Based Methods

This method is best used when you have issues related to classification and regression. Issues can be related to the segmentation of the predictor space into building simpler regions. Since there is a rule set for splitting the predictor space, you can decide and summarize that into a tree. This is known as the decision-tree method. We have a separate chapter for understanding the essence and role of a decision tree in data science. We have listed some common tree methods to ease your efforts using the same:

Bagging

Bagging helps to produce extra training data from the first or initial data or dataset, which results in the reduction of the variation of the prediction. When this is performed multiple times, in other words, repetition steps are performed, it produces a multi-step of similar carnality. It works inversely; as you increase the training set size, automatically the variance is decreased.

Boosting

This is also known as an averaging technique. In this method, the outcome of different models is computed to get the average of the results through a weighted average technique. By predicting and determining the merits and demerits of this technique, it is possible to develop an excellent predictive force that can be applied in a large amount of input data.

Random Forest

The algorithm used in the Random Forest Technique represents the famous Bagging Algorithm. The development of random bootstrap samples of the training sets is possible using this algorithm. Not limited to bootstrap, it is also possible to build a random subset of features that are generally used to train the individual trees. In bagging, a full set of features is assigned to each tree due to this random feature selection. Moreover, you can get better predictive performance by making the trees more independent of each other than using a normal bagging method.

8. Support Vector Machines (SVM)

The support vector machine is placed next to the supervised learning models in Machine Learning. This method is a type of Machine Learning. Alternatively, it is used to calculate hyperplane in higher dimensions such as 2D and 3D. A hyperplane explains about the dimensional side of the data. It is defined as a p-1 dimensional subspace of a p dimensional space that is used to predict the differences between two classes of points that have the maximum margin. Generally, the margin is optimized in this type. The data points that lie on either side of the hyperplane are known as support vectors. There are certain situations where it is not possible to separate the data; in such cases, the points are to be defined to a much higher dimensional space where you can apply linear separation. The problem that consists of multiple classes can be distributed into one-versus-one binary classification problems.

9. The Unsupervised Learning

In unsupervised learning, the data and group of data are not known. The patterns of the provided data are to be determined by the learning algorithms. Previously, we have seen an example of unsupervised learning, i.e., clustering. In clustering, different data sets are grouped into groups of closely related datasets.

Principal Component Analysis

Previously we have seen the principal component regression. Now let us look at the Principal Component Analysis. The generation of the least dimensional representation of any data set is possible by this method. Defining a certain set of linear properties having maximum variance and that are mutually unrelated results in a data set. This is important from a learning perspective to understand the latent interaction in unsupervised learning.

Hierarchical Clustering

This is a special type of clustering that develops a cluster tree by having a multilevel hierarchy of clusters.

K-means Clustering

K-means clustering is used to partition the data into K clusters depending upon the distance of the cluster from the center of the centroid. This clustering is a base of the statistical techniques that assist a data science program manager. It helps to develop a better skill set of what is happening other than data science Terms. Understanding basic terms of data science like algorithms, statistics, probability, etc. Are very important that would help in a better understanding of data science.

Overview of Data Modeling

Data Modeling is a crucial aspect of data science. It is the most appealing methodology, which is used and rewarded by most of the basic learners of data science. Data Modeling has received the most attention than any other process defined in data science. It has various functions to work with; one of them may be applying a function to a given class of a package. Making a model strong, reliable, and robust is what we get from data modeling. It is also associated with the building of information or data feature set. This process includes various functions that ensure proper and accurate handling of the data in the best possible way.

Robust Data Model

We learned about the designing of the data or dataset. But how would you produce the data? It is done by the robust data Model and should have good performance depending on different metrics. It depends on multiple metrics, as a simple metric may have some problems in designing the model because there are multiple aspects of the classification problems. Sensitivity analysis can be another important aspect of data science modeling. Sensitivity refers to a condition where if the input is meant to change slightly, then the output is changed considerably. Such inconsistency should not be there; hence, it checks for sensitivity also equally important to have a robust model. To end with interpretability, which is not possible in certain instances, but it turns out to be an essential aspect of data science. It refers to the interpretation of the result and the easiness of doing so. There is a technique known as a black box that is used to control the sensitivity. But it is somewhat hard to interpret because of the black box technique. It is recommended that you may go for a relatively interpretable model to defend the output from others.

Overview of Data Featurization

Data featurization is the next step after data modeling. We got an overview of how to model data efficiently. Now, let us go in deep about data Featurization. For any model to work best, it is highly recommended that it must have information that has rich sets of features. Before proceeding to the development of the data, it must be cleaned for certain purposes. Cleaning of data includes fixing issues with either of the two viz. The datasets or the data points, filling missing values wherever it is possible and in some situations removing noisy elements. Normalization would be the first step while you add variables in the model. It is done using the linear transformation method, making sure that the variables rotate around a given range. Usually, normalization is enough for turning variables into features if they are cleaned at the first step. Another process of featurization can be Binning. The binning process can be briefly described as the building of nominal variables, which are further divided into distinct binary features that are finally applied to the data model. Lastly, there are some reduction methods that are useful in building a feature set. Going through this, we must check out some important considerations in data Featurization.

Important Considerations

To add value to the data modeling, a data scientist must be able to consider certain important features apart from the basic attributes of the data science Modeling. This important consideration includes in-depth testing using specialized sampling, sensitivity analysis, and various aspects of the model performance to improvise any performance aspect belonging to data science Modeling.

The Future of data science and Predictive Modeling

There is no rocket science to know that how important is predictive analysis in the field of data science. The new algorithm-based firms have given us a direction on how to predict and find the outcome from a given data. All the use cases of data science and predictive modeling appear like having a tour – planning of tools to help customers better understand and define locations, dates, hotel needs, and other factors that impact travel details. These products have stepped forward towards a user-friendly data science tool that can change you into a data scientist.

From Predictive to Prescriptive

Earlier data scientists used predictive techniques, but gradually they are turning their face towards the prescriptive technique, which is a practical application. In the predictive phase, there were some historical data that predicted the probabilities of future outcomes, whereas prescriptive deals with the assumption that an active human agent may affect outcomes positively. Let us look at some definitions.

Ø Descriptive analytics

The initial stage of business analytics where historical data and performance is looked upon

Ø Predictive analytics

The second stage of business analytics, where the best course of action is chosen.

Ø Prescriptive analytics

This is the final three-stage business analytics, where the best course of action is taken by considering the action course that is chosen earlier.

The main reason for turning to prescriptive technique is that it helps uplifting of the model to have a chance to convert a lead for the given offer. To illustrate, to check if the company sends a sign-on bonus to see how it affects the chances of the employee to accept the job. This way leads to the proactive planning of the organization. On the other hand, such decisions create a line between machine and human interactions. Traditional predictive models were providing insights to the end-users about the likelihood of an event. It was in the hands of humans to decide what can they do with this information. However, the uplifting predictive model is also effective to determine the events of the outcome if you are given a course of action and asked to determine the events.

This method is especially important when you prepare a model and predict outcomes regarding politics, marketing, retail, medical, donations, etc.

Data Science Converging with AI

Artificial Intelligence has taken a full-fledged turn in the field of data science. Artificial Intelligence has two applications: Deep Learning and Machine Learning. Both of the applications affect heavily on the practice of data science. Mainly Machine learning is used in abundance in data science. AI tools help in the data gathering process and go even in-depth to analysis and organize the data into solutions and designs. For example, an Auto Cad engineer uses techniques to produce 3-Dimensional structures using Artificial Intelligence. AI can also be used in various projects, including model designing, chatbot, etc. The main feature, while doing this type of project, is not limited to create designs. Also, it creates different sets of datasets depending upon the structure and proposed solutions. Moreover, it allows designers to develop some prototypes that are focused mainly on customized problems/issues. Tools like this to be applied and used in the future must have a strict analytical function in data science; that will deliver insights and recommendations to products and Research and Development applications. Not only these tools perform tasks that a human does but also ensures effectiveness. Such Machines can predict insights, emotions that a human can feel. For example, Google Alexa, which runs on AI technology that analyses sound. Also, a few types of equipment that identifies human emotions.

End of Human-Driven data science

The latest technologies are growing at a faster pace, and they are being adopted everywhere, which will eventually lead to the end of the practice of asking any expert for any solution. All the solutions would be given by the Machine itself using AI technology. On the other hand, deep learning technology is recognized as the best technology having a neural network used to analyze end-to-end work. It will lead to automation in the near future, and the work of data scientists may reduce considerably. It is predicted that in the coming few decades, everything would be automated and stored in the cloud removing manual human efforts. A complete guide on Machine Learning and Deep Learning: Working with Neural Networks is explained in the upcoming chapters. You will have a brief overview of the complete working of such a technology, how to implement it, and when to implement it to produce more accurate results.

Chapter 5

Defining Data Science Tools

A lot of tools for processing data are available. Simply put, data analysis is a methodology requiring inspection, cleansing, transformation, and modeling of data. Its purpose is to discover vital information, the end result, a proper interpretation, and decipher a proper mode of action. This chapter gives you an idea about the best tools and techniques that data scientists use for data analysis.

Open Source Data Tools

Openrefine

Openrefine was earlier known as Google Refine. This tool is found to be most efficient when working with disorganized datasets. This enables data scientists to clean and put the data into a different format. It also allows the data scientist to integrate different datasets (external and internal). Google refine is a great tool for large-scale data exploration, enabling the user to discover the data patterns easily.

Orange

It is an open-source data visualization and analysis tool designed and meant for those people who do not have expertise in data science. It helps the user to build an interactive workflow that can be used for analysis and visualization of data, using a simple interactive workflow and an advanced toolbox. The output of this tool differs from the mainstream scatter plots, bar charts, and dendrograms.

Knime

Knime is another open-source solution tool that enables the user to explore data and interpret the hidden insights effectively. One of its good attributes is that it contains more than 1000 modules along with numerous examples to help the user to understand the applications and effective use of the tool. It is equipped with the most advanced integrated tools with some complex algorithms.

R-programming

R-programing is the most common and widely used tool. It has become a standard tool for programming. R is a free open source software that any user can install, use, upgrade, modify, clone, and even resell. It can easily and effectively be used in statistical computing and graphics. It is made in a way that is compatible with any type of operating system like Windows, macOS platforms, and UNIX. It is a high-performance language that lets the user manage big data. Since it is free and is regularly updated, it makes technological projects cost-effective. Along with data Mining, it lets the user apply their statistical and graphical knowledge, including common tests like a statistical test, clustering, and linear, non-linear modeling.

Rapidminer

Rapidminer is similar to KNIME with respect to dealing with visual programming for data modeling, analysis, and manipulation. It helps to improve the overall yield of data science project teams. It offers an open-source platform that permits Machine Learning, model deployment, and data preparation. It is responsible for speeding up the development of an entire analytical workflow, right from the steps of model validation to deployment.

Pentaho

Pentaho tackles issues faced by the organization concerning its ability to accept values from another data source. It is responsible for simplifying data preparation and data blending. It also provides tools used for analysis, visualization, reporting, exploration, and prediction of data. It lets each member of a team assign the data meaning.

Weka

Weka is another open-source software that is designed with a view of handling machine-learning algorithms to simplify data Mining tasks. The user can use these algorithms directly in order to process a data set. Since it is implemented in JAVA programming, it can be used for developing a new Machine Learning scheme. It lets easy transition into the field of data science owing to its simple Graphical User Interface. Any user acquainted with JAVA can invoke the library into their code.

The nodexl

The nodexl is open-source software, data visualization, and analysis tool that is capable of displaying relationships in datasets. It has numerous modules, like social network data importers and automation.

Gelphi

Gelphi is an open-source visualization and network analysis tool written in Java language.

Talend

Talend is one of the leading open-source software providers that most data-driven companies go for. It enables the customers to connect easily irrespective of the places they're at.

Data Visualization

Data Wrapper

It is an online data-visualization software that can be used to build interactive charts. Data in the form of CSV, Excel, or PDF can be uploaded. This tool can be used to generate a map, bar, and line. The graphs created using this tool have ready to use embed codes and can be uploaded on any website.

Tableau Public

Tableau Public is a powerful tool that can create stunning visualizations that can be used in any type of business. Data insights can be identified with the help of this tool. Using visualization tools in Tableau Public, a data scientist can explore data prior to processing any complex statistical process.

Infogram

Infogram contains more than 35 interactive charts and 500 maps that allow the user to visualize data. It can make various charts like a word cloud, pie, and bar.

Google Fusion Tables

Google Fusion Tables is one of the most powerful data analysis tools. It is widely used when an individual has to deal with massive datasets.

Solver

The solver can support effective financial reporting, budgeting, and analysis. You can see a button that will allow you to interact with the profit-making data in a company.

Sentiment Tools

Opentext

Identification and evaluation of expressions and patterns are possible in this specialized classification engine. It carries out analysis at various levels: document, sentence, and topic level.

Trackur

Trackur is an automated sentiment analysis software emphasizing a specific keyword that is tracked by an individual. It can draw vital insights by monitoring social media and mainstream news. In short, it identifies and discovers different trends.

Opinion Crawl

Opinion Crawl is also an online sentiment analysis software that analyses the latest news, products, and companies. Every visitor is given the freedom to access Web sentiment in a specific topic. Anyone can participate in a topic and receive an assessment. A pie chart reflecting the latest real-time sentiment is displayed for every topic. Different concepts that people relate to are represented by various thumbnails and cloud tags. The positive and negative effect of the sentiments is also displayed. Web crawlers search the up-to-date content published on recent subjects and issues to create a comprehensive analysis.

Data Extraction Tools

Content Grabber

Content Grabber is a tool designed for organizations to enable data mining and save the data in a specific format like CSV, XML, and Excel reports. It also has a scripting and editing module, making it a better option for programming experts. Individuals can also utilize C#, VB.NET to debug, and write script information.

IBM Cognos Analytics

IBM Cognos Analytics was developed after Cognos Business Intelligence. It is used for data visualization in the BI product. It is developed with a Web-based interface. It covers a variety of modules, such as data governance, strong analytics, and management. The integration of data from different sources to make reports and visualizations is possible using this tool.

Sage Live

Sage Live is a cloud-based accounting platform that can be used in small and mid-sized types of businesses. It enables the user to create invoices, bill payments using smartphones. This is a perfect tool if you wish to have a data visualization tool supporting different companies, currencies, and banks.

Gawk GNU

Gawk GNU allows the user to utilize a computer without software. It interprets unique programming language enabling the users to handle simple-data reformatting Jobs. Following are its main attributes:

> ➤ It is not procedural. It is data-driven.

> ➤ Writing programs is easy.

> ➤ Searching for a variety of patterns from the text units.

Graphlab creates

Graphlab can be used by data scientists as well as developers. It enables the user to build state-of-the-art data products using Machine Learning to create smart applications.

The attributes of this tool are the Integration of automatic feature engineering, Machine Learning visualizations, and model selection to the application. It can identify and link records within and across data sources. It can simplify the development of Machine Learning models.

Netlink Business Analytics

Netlink Business Analytics is a comprehensive on-demand solution providing the tool. You can apply it through any simple browser or company-related software. Collaboration features also allow the user to share the dashboards among teams. Features can be customized as per sales and complicated analytic capability, which is based on inventory forecasting, fraud detection, sentiment, and customer churn analysis.

Apache Spark

Apache Spark is designed to run-in memory and real-time.

The top 5 data analytics tools and techniques

Visual analytics

Different methods that can be used for data analysis are available. These methods are possible through integrated efforts involving human interaction, data analysis, and visualization.

Business Experiments

All the techniques that are used in testing the validity of certain processes are included in Business Experiments AB testing, business experiments, and the experimental design.

Regression Analysis

Regression Analysis allows the identification of factors that make two different variables related to each other.

Correlation Analysis

Correlation Analysis is a statistical technique that detects whether a relationship exists between two different variables.

Time Series Analysis

Time Series analysis gathers data at specific time intervals. Identifying changes and predicting future events in a retrospective manner is possible using this.

Chapter 6

Basic Statistics Concepts
Data Scientists

W hile opting for data science, one of the main concepts which should be known to anyone in the fundamentals of data science. Fundamentals include statistics that are further classified as distributions, dimensionality reality, probability, etc. One should be familiar with the fundamentals while thinking of getting into data science. Let us take a look at the statistical concepts.

Statistics

Statistics is one of the most important aspects of data science. Thus, it can be said that statistics is a powerful tool while performing the art of data science. Then you may wonder what statistics actually are. Statistics can be defined as high-level mathematics, which is used to perform any technical analysis of data. For example, a bar chart or line graph may give you a basic visualization of the data and high-level information, but statistics have an additional advantage of "more information," i.e., We are able to work on the data in a deeper sense and targeted way, which can be referred to as "information-driven approach". The Math involved in this approach results in concrete and accurate conclusions, which eventually reduces your efforts in estimating or guesstimating data.

By the use of statistics, we are able to gain deep-level and more refined insights about the structural view of the data. The structural view helps us in identifying and getting more information by optimally applying other data science techniques. There are five basic statistics concepts that a data scientist must be familiar with, and they must know how to apply them in the most effective way!

Statistical Features

The most common and used concept of statistics is Statistical features. You will work with many things like bias, variance, mean, median, percentiles, graphs, and tables. Statistics is probably the first stats technique you will work with while exploring a data or dataset. Understanding and learning statistics is more or less easy for a beginner!

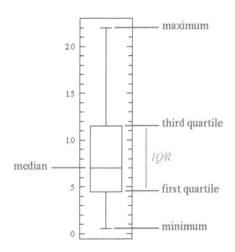

[source - http://www.physics.csbsju.edu]

Observe the above figure - The line cutting the middle is known as the median value of the data. Sometimes, there is confusion between a median and a mean. Median is usually used over a mean value as it is more robust, relating to the outlier surfaces. Now, as per figure, it is divided into three quartiles; The first quartile is approximately at the 25th percentile, i.e., 25% of the data points are placed below that value. Similarly, the third quartile is approximately at the 75th percentile i.e., 75% of the data are placed below that value. The minimum and maximum values represent the lower and upper limits of the data range, respectively.

The above plot defines the statistical features:

Ø If there are many values in a small range with most of the similar data points, the box plot will represent as "short."

Ø If there is a wide range of values with most of the different data points, the box plot will represent as "tall."

Ø Depending upon the position of the median, it can be said that if the median value is near the bottom limit, then most of the data would have lower values. Inversely, if the median value is near the upper limit, then most of the data would have higher values. To sum up: you will find skewed data if the median value is not exactly at the center of the box plot.

Ø Is the tail very long? This indicates that the data has a very high standard deviation and variance i.e., The values are scattered and highly varying. Imagine you have the long tail bending towards only one side of the box and not on the other side, then your data may be varying in only that direction.

The above box plot example was quite simple to understand and calculate information from the same. Now let us have a look into some similar concepts in detail:

Probability Distributions

Probability can be defined as the occurrence of some percent change in an event. Usually, probability value is calculated or quantified between the standard range of 0 to 1. Where 0 indicates that the probability of occurrence of an event is not repetitive. Whereas, one indicates that the probability of occurrence of an event is very repetitive. A probability distribution is a function that represents all the probabilities of possible values in the model. Let us take a look at some common probability distribution patterns:

Uniform Distribution Pattern

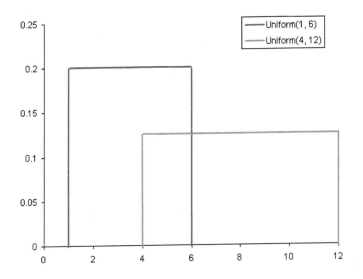

[source = https://miro.medium.com]

Uniform Distribution is the most simple and basic type of distribution. Observe the above figure for the X and Y coordinates and the points on the co-ordinates. This distribution has only one value that will occur in a certain range. Anything outside that value range would mean that the range is 0. It is also known as "on or off" distribution. We can categorize the values as 0 or the value. The variable other than zero may have multiple values between 0 to 1, but it can be visualization in a similar way as we did in the piecewise function of multiple uniform distributions.

Normal Distribution Pattern

Normal Distribution also referred to as a "Gaussian Distribution." It is defined by the mean value and the standard deviation that is shown. The initial value is responsible for shifting and adjusting the distribution spatially, whereas the spread is controlled by the standard deviation. The highlighting difference in this distribution is that the standard deviation is the same in all the directions regardless of the change in the mean value. With Gaussian distribution, we can understand the overall average value of the information or data. The data spread of the model viz. We can also identify the range of the data spread, which may be in a concentrated format of the data revolving to the few values, or it can have a wider range that is spread over the values.

Poisson Distribution

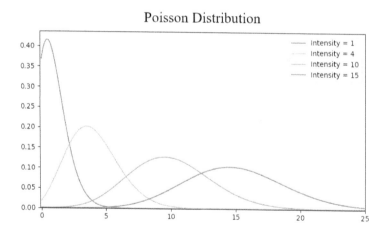

[source = https://miro.medium.com]

The above graph depicts a Poisson Distribution, where all the signals are in the continuous form with variable intensities. Poisson Distribution can be compared to the uniform distribution as it is very much similar to that; the exception is only the skewness. Skew or skewness can be defined as "neither parallel nor perpendicular to a specified or implied line." If the skew value is less, then it will have a uniform spread in all the direction like the normal distribution. On the other hand, if the skewness is high, the distribution would be scattered in different positions. It might be concentrated in one position, or it can be scattered all over the graph.

This is an overview of the commonly used distribution pattern. But distributions are not limited to these three; there are many more distributions that are used in data science. Out of these three, Gaussian distribution can be used with many algorithms, whereas choosing an algorithm in Poisson distribution must be a careful discussion due to its skewness feature.

Dimensionality Reduction

Dimensionality Reduction can be somewhat instinctive to understand. In data science, we would be given a dataset, and by the use of the Dimensionality Reduction technique, we will have to reduce the dimensions of the data.

Imagine you have been given a dataset cube of 1000 data points, and it's a 3-Dimension cube. Now you might think that computing 1000 data points can be an easy process, but at a larger scale, it might give birth to many problems and complexity. Now by using the dimensionality reduction technique, if we look at the data in 2-Dimension, then it is easy to re-arrange the colors into categories. This will reduce the size of the data points from 1000 to maybe 100 if you categorize colors in 10 groups. Computing 100 data points are much easier than earlier 1000 data points. In a rare case, these 100 data points can also be reduced to 10 data points by the dimensional reduction technique by identifying color similarity and grouping similar color shades in a group. This is possible only in the 1-Dimension view. This technique helps in a big computational saving.

Feature Pruning

Feature pruning is another technique of performing dimensionality reduction. As we saw that we reduce the points in the earlier technique, here, we can reduce the number of features that are less important or not important to our analysis. For illustration, while working on any data set, we may come across 20 features; 15 of them might have a high correlation with the output, whereas five may not having any correlation, or maybe they may have a very low correlation. Then we may want to remove that five features by feature pruning technique to reduce unwanted elements as well as reduce the computing time and effort, taking into consideration that the output remains unaffected.

Over and Under Sampling

Over and Under Sampling techniques are the classification techniques used for the perfect classification of the problems. Possibilities are there whenever we try to classify datasets. For example, imagine we have 2000 data points in Class 1 but only 200 data points in Class 2. This will require a lot of Machine Learning Techniques to model the data and make predictions upon our observations! Here, over and under sampling, comes into the picture. Look at the below representation.

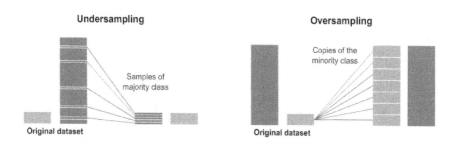

Look at the image carefully; it can be stated that on both sides, the blue class has a higher number of samples compared to the orange class. In such a case, we have two predetermined, pre-processing options that can ease to predict the result.

Defining Under-Sampling

Under-sampling means the selection of few data from the major class, utilizing as many data points as the minor class is equipped with. This selection is performed to maintain the probability level of the class.

Defining Oversampling

Oversampling means creating copies of the data points from the minor class to level the number of data points in the major class. The copies are made considering that the distribution of the minor class is maintained.

Bayesian Statistics

Before understanding Bayesian Statistics, we need to know why frequency analysis can't be applied here. You can understand from the following example.

Imagine you are playing the dice game. What are the chances of you rolling a perfect 6? You would probably say that the chance would be 1 in 6, right? In the event, if we perform a frequency analysis technique here, we would catch that if someone rolled the dice for 10,000 times, then you may come out with 1 in 6 estimates. But if you are given a dice that is loaded to land always on 6, it would be easy to put six at every time. Since frequency analysis takes the prior data into account, it fails sometimes. Bayesian Statistics take into account the evidence.

Baye's Theorem

Let us learn the meaning of the theorem. The capacity P(H) is the recurrence examination. Given our earlier information, what is the likelihood of our occasion happening? The P(E|H) in our condition is known as the probability and is basically the likelihood that our proof is right, given the data from our recurrence examination. For instance, if you think of rolling the dice 5,000 times and the initial 1000 times the dice rolled out to be a 6, then it is pretty clear that the dice is having a perfect six only. Here, the P(E) is the likelihood that the real proof is valid.

In the event that the performed recurrence examination is generally excellent, at that point, you can be certain that the dice is stacked with an impeccable 6. Yet, you should likewise mull over the proof of the stacked dice, regardless of whether it's actual or not founded on its earlier information and the recurrence investigation you just performed. Each and everything is taken into consideration in this theorem. Bayesian Theorem is useful when you are in doubt that the prior data is not sufficient to predict the result. These statistical concepts are very useful for an aspiring data scientist.

Chapter 7

Understanding Probability & Data Visualization

Introduction to Probability

In the earlier chapter, we took a brief tour of probability. But it is important to know the inside out of the probability to excel in Data Science. Having knowledge of probability and mathematics solves your 50% of the problems while working for a project. Probability is easy to understand if you think of examples revolving around you & link them with probability. One of the best examples could be a dice game. The probability that a perfect six would come in certain turns. It is made of universal sets of assumptions. Suppose you want to roll 4 on the dice in your 50 attempts. Then what will be the probability of getting only 4 in 50 turns? This is known as an event where you calculate the probability. Normally, the probability is denoted by "P". For certain events, the probability will be denoted by P (E). Let us see how probability is used in Data Science.

Dependent & Independent Events

Let us consider two events, namely A & B. Events A & B are said to be dependent if event A can predict the information that event B would be producing. For example, if you flip a coin & you know the outcome of the next step, then they are dependent events.

Conversely, when it is not possible for Event A to predict the information of what Event B would be producing on the next step, then they are known as independent events. For example, if you flip a coin & you get a tail on the first attempt, it will not give any information about the outcome of the second flip. The next flip might be a head or a tail. Such events are known as independent events. In Mathematics, events A and B are called independent only if their independent probability products equal the probability of both events taking place.

$$P (A, B) = P (A) P (B)$$

In the above example, the probability that it will be only Head is 0.5. Whereas, the probability of both the events is 0.25. Then the probability that it will be Tail is 0.

Conditional Probability

If the probability of any one of the events is not zero, then it is said to be conditional on the other event. Suppose Event B is not zero, whereas Event is A is zero, then Event A is said to be conditional on B. It is given by the formula:

$$P (A/B) = P (A,B) / P (B)$$

$$P (A,B) = P (A/B) P (B)$$

If both the events are independent then,

$$P (A/B) = P (A)$$

The above expression clearly states that the occurrence of event B does not give any information about the occurrence of event A.

This case can be illustrated by an example of the garden having two unknown plants.

Assumptions can be made like:

➢ Both the plants are equally likely to be a flowering or non-flowering plant.

➢ The characteristics of the second plant does not depend on the characteristics of the first plant.

Hence, the event "non-flowering" will be having a probability of 0.25. Whereas, the event "one flowering, one non-flowering" will have a probability of 0.5. Lastly, the event "two non-flowering" will have a 0.25 probability. If you need to find the probability of whether "both plants are non-flowering" is conditional on the event "the older plant is non-flowering", you can use conditional probability technique.

Bayes' Theorem

We have studied Bayes' Theorem in the earlier chapters. It is basically used when you are required to reverse the conditional probability. We saw the case where the probability of event B is conditional on event A. But what about the reverse conditions? Bayes' Theorem helps us to understand the reverse condition of the probability. For example, suppose 1 out of 100 students have failed in the examination. There will be an exam for testing where the student has passed the exam. The test will display "pass" if the student is passed or "failed" if the student has not passed the exam. From the example, it will display "passed" for 99%. But by Bayes' Theorem, the probability of the students failed conditional on the positive testing will be 0.98%. This is less than 1% of the students who have failed.

Random Variables

A random variable is a positively valued variable that is associated with a probability distribution model. Considering the example of flipping the coin, then the random variable is 1 when it is a tail & 0 when it is a Head. You can calculate the number of heads & tails for a selected value range of maybe (10) where the probability of each number flipped would be likely equal. There is a similarity between the two probability values when flipped. The variable value will be 1 having a probability of 0.5, whereas the variable value will be 0 having the probability of 0.5. For a specific range of variable values, considering a range of 10 variable values from 0 to 9, the probability distribution for all the values would be 0.5. This is known as the average of its weighted value calculated as per their probabilities. Finally, we can say that the flipping of the coin variable will have an expected value of $0.5 = 1/2 (= 0 * 1/2 + 1 * 1/2)$. The range of 10 variable values will have an average value of 4.5. You can make use of conditional probability for calculating the probabilities of a specific range of variables or any random variable of similar or distinct events.

There are different probability distribution patterns, taking the same example of flipping a coin, we shall consider two different distributions i.e. Continuous Distributions, & Normal Distributions. Later, we shall learn about the Central limit theorem that is very important to understand probability.

Continuous Distributions

Flipping of a coin refers to a distinct distribution. The probability outcomes in such cases are distinct. For example, there is a uniformity in assigning a weight for all the selected numbers, i.e. if the range of numbers is selected between 0 to 9, then the weight assigned to them is equal. Since there are numbers between the specific range, the weight assigned to the numbers can be zero or any similar number.

Normal Distribution

This is the most widely used distribution having two parameters: mean & deviation. The location of the centered variable & the width of the plane is determined by this mean & deviation, respectively.

The Central Limit Theorem

In the event, you will have to deal with a huge amount of data at a time. It becomes difficult to extract meaningful information from such huge datasets. Usually, data scientists pull out some amount of data to study & investigate further. However, a limited amount of data does not meet the required outcome. Some more data is looked upon & studied to get meaningful information. It becomes easy to predict the mean of the data with its median & mode. Then, you can plot any diagram from 7 QC tools; the best one is histogram to produce meaningful information & review the data.

Symmetrical Frequency Distribution

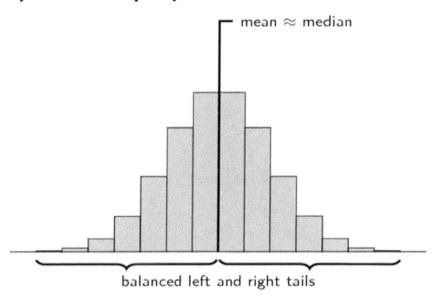

[source= https://www.siyavula.com]

From the above symmetrical frequency distribution figure, you can figure out that the left & right tails are balanced & symmetrical. The frequency is the highest at the median, whereas it falls at both the side corners. This suggests that when you will calculate the adequate amount of data from a huge database of data, you will get the average that would be similar to the average of the overall data where the median almost equals the mean of the data.

Normal Distribution

Normal Distribution is the most common & widely used distribution pattern. In the earlier chapters, we had a brief overview of this distribution. It also plays a role while dealing with probability. The normal distribution is known as "normal" as it is perfectly symmetrical to the mean of the data. The direction of the probabilities is also the same as that of the median. Refer to the below diagram for better understanding this.

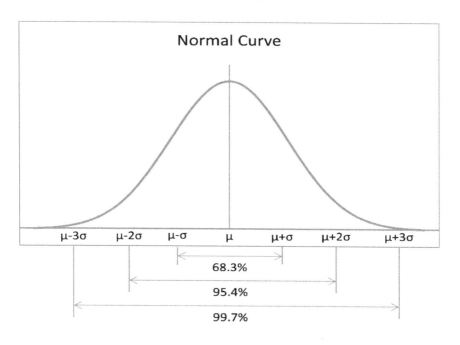

[source= https://www.syncfusion.com]

The figure depicts the standard working of the normal distribution. The area covered by the center curve is 1 & the value may change about the spread of the data. The standard deviation in % is specified for each area in the diagram. The probabilities nearest to the median have less deviation compared to the farthest probability value. As the probability value increases, the curve starts spreading in both directions equally, but it flatters further, as shown. When the deviation reaches almost 100%, the curve flattens totally. Similarly, we can say that when the standard deviation of the data is the lowest, it will touch the median. Conversely, when the standard deviation of the data is at its peak value, it will jump to the farthest position from the median.

An area in the Normal Distribution

Let us analyze which type of data is required in the area of normal distribution pattern. Consider you have certain data of healthy & non-healthy plants with you & you need to predict the probability of the healthy plants. Suppose the mean value (μ) of all the plants is 150 & assume the standard deviation to be equivalent to 15. This means that the healthy plants will be having the standard deviation tilted towards the mean. So the upper & lower limits would be 165 & 135 respectively. When you calculate the percentage deviation of such a curve, you will get an approximate to 68% curve.

Z scores

In statistics, the probability value will be between 0 & 1 & it will deviate as per the situation & model of the data. The probability value will never equal to 1σ or 2σ from the mean distance. Then you may wonder, what is Z score? Z score is the calculated distance that depends upon the number & value of the standard deviation &

the mean of the data, respectively. There are positive & negative values of Z; positive value refers to more deviation from the mean, whereas the negative value refers to less deviation from the mean.

Data Visualization

Pictorial depiction always simplifies the process of understanding and discovering important data insights. They're helpful when there is a need for relating hundreds of variables with each other. A large amount of data is generated every day by all the companies. Every employee needs to handle specific datasets. They need to be particular about the data set they pick up in order to make better decisions for effective work. Irrespective of the size of the data, mastering important relationships is through rigorous analysis and simple visualizations. Leaving out on any minute details can lead to misinterpretation of the actual results. Displaying the outcome in a simple manner enables readers to explore the data and raise queries regarding the same. This helps everybody in the organization to reach a conclusion and gain insights into the data quickly. Standard things one needs to consider to develop significant visuals are data type, data size, and column composition. One of the greatest challenges faced by data scientists while dealing with large datasets is determining an appropriate method to use to display data. Current society mandates the use of visualization and interaction. So, creating graphs that allow readers to visualize it in smartphones while having the freedom to interact with data in real-time has become the norm. Take an example of SAS Visual Analytic Support where it supports many business customers to gather some output without them having the Data science skills. Based on the type of data highlighted, intelligent and auto-charting tools have been used for the creation of the best visuals. Using these tools, it has become possible to identify the relevant findings without writing the algorithms.

Dealing with Charts
Charting

Line Charts

Line charts help in finding the relationship between variables. It is rendered best when you have a huge amount of data items, and you need to make comparisons between them. It has stack lines for different variables and values. It is used to display the trends. However, again, based on the number of data items, the type of visuals to be used will be decided.

Bar Charts

Bar charts enable the user to make comparisons between quantities of different groups. Values from a specific category are displayed using vertical or horizontal bars whose lengths are proportionate to the values they are assigned. If the data is spread over a large range and the differences between points are more, it becomes very easy to read a bar graph. However, in cases when the difference in values is less, it becomes difficult to compare bars. So in order to avoid any hassles, you can assign different colors to different categories.

There are various types of bar charts, like a progressive Bar chart. The progressive Bar chart is used to show the increment or decrement in measure of an original value during a transaction. The working of the bar graph can be explained as the first bar starts from the initial value & each subsequent bar starts from the end of the first bar. Generally, such bars display the length as well as the direction to include the magnitude.

Scatter Plots

A two-dimensional plot describing the shared difference of two data items is a scatter plot. Each observation is marked by a scatter mark. The value of the data item is reflected by the position of the marker. Creating a relationship between x and y-axis becomes easier using these plots. There is a correlation between the dependency of every variable that may affect each other. It is one of the best tools to easily visualize the relationships in data. Correlation and regression can be used for statistical analysis via these plots. Correlation helps in identifying the extent of relatedness amongst all the variables in plot. Whereas, regression helps in defining relationships between the 2 variables. Understanding the overall spread of the data and the distribution becomes really easy with scatter plots. It is beneficial to use when you have a large number of data points.

Bubble Plots

Scatter plots with bubbles as the markers are nothing but bubble plots. A bubble plot enables the individual to reveal the relationship between three measurements. The plot axes highlight the data points if you have 2 measurements. Applying color to illustrate extra measurement and animating the bubbles help in effectively analyzing the changes in the data. Each of the maps is represented in a specific geographic location, and a geo bubble map is placed over a geographic map.

Pie and Donut Charts

Pie charts and donut charts, both help in creating comparisons between parts. Comparing visual angles and estimation of areas with naked eyes isn't very evident. So, comparing data that is similar in size using these graphs becomes difficult to read. You should analyze how a donut and a pie chart works before making use of these charts. The amount of space that a chart needs to size a report reveals the efficiency of a pie chart. Most of these charts require additional space owing to their circular shape.

How to Visualize Big Data

Specific problems are presented by big data. It is extremely useful to use charts when you want to visualize data because of the speed, size, and diversity of the data. Velocity, Volume, and Variety are the basic building blocks of Big Data. A creative approach to handle issues regarding Big data visualization is taken care of by SAS visual analytics. Integration of SAS Analytics and in-memory capabilities are used to reveal new ways of representing and analyzing data.

Dealing with Large Data Volumes

Data scientists do really have a hard time when they want to present the results of a data exploration and analysis. Working with a large amount of generated data belonging to different categories, only numerical values will not be enough for actually gaining meaningful insights into the data. This makes it extremely important for them to use visualization tools. Gone are the days when plain visuals were of great importance. Smart problems require smart solutions. In this era of the smart world, dynamic interactive data points and visuals are of equal importance. Based on the size and type of data, the auto-charting function built-in SAS Visual Analytics reviews data. Business analytics and employees can use this tool with the utmost ease. A hierarchy of data and its interactive exploration can take place in every possible manner using this tool. The volume of data poses a problem for traditional architecture and the software. It may not define such a huge size of the data immediately. Thus, this type of application may fail to work. One solution for overcoming this problem is binning. Gathering data from both axes to visualize the big data is a crucial step in binning. A box plot describes a geographical display of five statistics, namely medial, lower quartile, upper quartile, maximum, and minimum. These values are critical when you wish to put forward a summary to define the distribution of a set of data. Data scientists utilize these box plots to identify abnormal points called outliers.

Box plots are preferred over others by data scientists because it helps in identifying outliers (abnormal points in the data). This data proportion is not hard to notice for traditional datasets. However, for those working with a vast data set, it can be very hard to identify.

How to Visualize Semi-Structured and Unstructured Data

Be it structured or semi-structured data, they'll both require data visualization techniques. This poses a challenge for the data scientist. The frequency of the words can be indicated by the application of a word cloud visual. This can either be low or high. Word clouds are important in the classification and creation of associations in the SAS Visual Analytics. Based on the way the words are used, these words are further categorized.

Data Scientists also visualize semi-structured data using network diagrams. These diagrams are specially designed to establish relationships between individuals by examining the nodes. Network diagrams can be used in different disciplines and applications. For example, businesses that analyze social networks discover interactions with customers.

Chapter 8

Machine Learning with Artificial Neural Networks

Do you know how does a computer protects you from spam emails and malicious phishing links? The computer does help us stay safe from such trojans. In the modern era, computers are becoming more intelligent due to human interference. You can teach a computer to identify persons in the images, pictures, etc. You will think that this is merely impossible or very difficult to do so. But let me help you with the fact that this is possible. You should add a new skill in your toolkit i.e., Machine Learning. We will learn about Machine Learning and the Need for Machine Learning. Later, going into deep, we will see Deep Learning, i.e., Artificial Neural Networks.

What is Machine Learning?

Machine Learning is a scientific study of algorithms and statistics that works on different patterns and interferences without any specific instruction. Machine learning is a subset of Artificial Intelligence. Machine Learning is broadly divided into two subcategories, i.e., supervised learning and unsupervised learning.

To start with Machine Learning, a general-purpose algorithm is developed by the experts to ensure it can be applied to large classes of learning problems. When you want to solve any specific problem, you will just load the algorithm with the required data. By default, you will be programming a code. Generally, the computer will make data as its initial source of information and will start comparing its output to the desired output that you need. If it is not achieved, then the computer will correct it until you get the desired output. The computer loaded with specific algorithms thinks similarly to human thought. If you add more data to the computer, the computer gives better outcomes. Machine learning has many day-to-day applications.

Importance of Machine Learning

In the modern era, machine learning has become the basic need for data science. It is used almost everywhere; then, it may be evaluation, processing, learning, etc. of the data model. It helps in solving various problems that Image Processing, computer vision, Energy production for load, computations in algorithm trading, credit scoring, recognition of voice through NLP, and many more industries such as aerospace, automotive, and manufacturing. Machine learning has wide applications in almost all types of companies.

As we have seen, machine-learning algorithms are way different from the statistical methodology, and also it identifies the nature but meaningful patterns to evaluate the information and make accurate decisions. Some critical decisions where machine learning is used are medical diagnoses, stocks, and trading, weather forecasting. Such decisions are taken daily by the teams. For example, the weather forecasting requires very accurate prediction, with the help of machine learning applications, it is possible to predict tomorrow's weather today. It analyses the data and makes possible predictions, but the most accurate is passed to the learner. Also, the second example is about list searching on Google about movies. If you type a keyword, it will suggest various options, but even search engines make a smart analysis and predict the best list that matches your keyword and displays the result.

When is it Right to Apply Machine Learning?

But you might think that when it is the right time to apply machine-learning techniques. Not every time you can opt for ML, but only when you are working on complex tasks. Normal tasks can be evaluated by normal statistical analysis. To get an overview of the applications, projects, categories where you can apply machine-learning techniques are Image Processing, Text Analysis, and Data Mining. Let us have a broad look over these categories.

A. Image Processing

Image processing is the process where you have to see the images, analyze them, and extract meaningful information by applying algorithms. Examples of Image processing can be Image Tagging, Optical Character Recognition.

➤ Image Tagging

In Image Tagging, an algorithm identifies the face. For example, on the iPhone there is a feature known as "face detection," the mobile will be unlocked only when it will recognize the face of the person who has initially locked the phone by registering his face.

➤ Optical Character Recognition

In OCR, the algorithms will change a scanned text document into its digital version. For example, if you upload an invoice on the system where OCR is already implemented. OCR will automatically check for the scanned text, and it will convert them into digital format.

B. Text Analysis

In-Text Analysis, the data is identified and classified from text documents like emails, documents, chats, etc. Examples are –

➤ Sentiment Analysis.

➤ Information Extraction.

➤ Spam filtering.

C. Data Mining

Data Mining process is used when you need to determine the predictions from any data. This seems to be a normal process, but it has the second side as well. The information that is extracted is very crucial and taken from a vast database. This will work in the row format where the training instances are recorded. Columns have some rules associated with them like association rules, Anomaly Detections, Predictions, etc.

➤ Association Rules

You can take an example of any e-commerce site. The biggies like Amazon, Walmart, etc. Determines the pattern of the product you bought and analyze your buying habits. Also, they add some discounts to such products. This is the best marketing strategy used by such e-commerce sites.

➤ Anomaly Detection

Anomaly Detection refers to the checking outliers. The best example can be credit card money fraud or theft. It is possible to identify the pattern of a transaction and the outlier from the user.

Steps in the Application of Machine Learning

1. Choose the Machine Learning Approach

Before choosing any steps to resolve the issue, you must be able to identify the problem and decide which Machine Learning technique is used. Query yourself about how are you going to deal with this problem? What technique will you be using? What type of algorithm will be required? Once you analyze this, it becomes simple to choose the correct approach for solving the problem.

2. Collect Data

After you decide your approach, you will start noting down the important data on the paper, but remember, recording and saving the files on the server or in an electronic format is always easy to store and retrieve. You can store in an SQL database or just record and save the files on the device.

3. Explore and Prepare Data

After you store the files or record it on your paper, you have to check the files for accuracy, and then you will prepare the data as per quality required. The effectiveness lies in the best quality of the data. This method requires human intervention to maintain the quality of the data. Once you prepare the data, it is the time when you explore it and apply it to the data model.

4. The Training Model on the Data

In this step, you will feed accurate data into the data model. The Machine learning tasks identify the suitable and correct algorithm for you. A machine-learning learner is the one who is trained on the algorithms to adjust the data in the model in the best possible way.

5. Evaluate the Performed of a Model

At every step, the accuracy of the data must not be altered. The accuracy must be maintained. While evaluating the data model, it is necessary to check the accuracy again. The learner must be able to generate the best possible way in which algorithms learn from the experience.

6. *Enhance Model Performance*

Till now, we saw the outline of how to select the machine learning approach till feeding the data in the data model with accuracy. But these steps also need enhancement, and they must be completed at a faster pace. You are required to make use of advanced techniques and mechanisms. Once you have ensured quality, you can deploy it for the required task. These models are useful in the generation of prediction scores, novel data values, and useful insights for random purposes. Also, you must be able to track the failures, if any, in the model.

Use of Machine Learning in Data Science

Although regression and classification form the base of the data science, to understand this concept, it is required to understand Machine Learning. In data science, at almost all the steps, Machines Learning is useful and utilized. Since it is mainly linked with data-modeling, but it is used across all the systems in data science. To embark with the data preparation phase, it is required to use ML and process towards the data modeling phase that requires qualitative raw data to start-off. Take an example of a text string, where you need to group the similar strings into a group and highlight non-similar strings; with the help of machine learning, you can easily differentiate the similar and non-similar stings and group accordingly.

When it becomes difficult to explore the data only with the help of charts and logics, algorithms can dig out the patterns with Machine

Learning. It is of no surprise that various Python libraries are developed for the same purpose!

Machine Learning with Python Tools

Python comes with a bundle of packages that can be used in the setting of Machine Learning. The Python ML ecosystem is divided into three main categories of packages:

- Packages used in simple tasks with a small amount of data that easily fit in the memory.

- Post the pro-typing optimization of coding that runs into memory.

- Working in Python with Big data Technologies.

Some various packages and Libraries are used to enhance the functionalities of coding. Some of them are scipy, numpy, Matplotlib, Pandas (High-performance package), Stats Models, Scikit-learn, Rpy2, NLTK (Natural Language Toolkit – focusing mainly on the text analytics).

Optimizing Operations

As your application enters the production server, you will require to work at a higher speed. The libraries listed below will help you to get high speed. This may involve connecting with Big data Infrastructures like Hadoop and Spark. Let's glance at the libraries quickly viz. Number and numbapro, pycuda, Cython or C Python

(C programming language with Python), Blaze, Display and ipcluster, PP, Pydoop, and Hadoop, pyspark, etc.

In data science, you may come across certain Tasks that are very complex to program, even by Machine learning such tasks are challenging. The tasks are "The tasks performed by Animals/Humans" and "Tasks performed beyond Human Capabilities." Let us understand what they mean.

Tasks Performed by Humans

Such tasks are normal tasks performed by humans in day-to-day life. But to plan and work on the tasks and how you can yield a well-defined program matter. Common examples are driving speech recognition and image understanding. In all these tasks, programs that learn from their experiences perform better, and results are outstanding. But initially, you may find it difficult to handle such common tasks if you do not have enough experience.

Tasks beyond Human Capabilities

Such tasks benefit from Machine Learning techniques that are related to very complex data sets; examples are turning medical archives into medical knowledge. Other examples can be weather predictions, analysis of genomic data, Web search engines, and electronic commerce. There is a large set of digital data available in the data storage that has a piece of meaningful information embedded in the data archives. These sets are very complex and very large to predict for humans. Due to cloud storage with unlimited memory capacity, meaningful patterns can be drawn from large sets using Machine Learning.

Machine Learning Tools

Machine learning tools offer a solution to such complex issues either by nature, or they interact with the adaptive changes of the environment. Application tools relating to Machine Learning that help to tackle such problems include handwritten text decoding program; program analysis like identifying different variations between the handwriting of different users. Other examples include spam detection programs, automatic change of nature of e-mail, and speech recognition.

Understanding Machine Learning

Not only learning Machine Learning, but any type of Learning is a wide domain with various strategies, programs, and analysis. Machine Learning is a subset of Artificial Intelligence, subdivided into Supervised Learning and Unsupervised Learning. Both categories work on different techniques and patterns. It is mainly related to the input and output of the information or the data. There are four parameters along which learning can be classified.

Supervised vs. Unsupervised Learning – You can divide the task considering the nature of the interaction between the learner and the environment. The first thing is to know what the difference between supervised and unsupervised learning is. Think of an example as learning to detect spam emails vs. detection of an anomaly. For spam email detection tasks, you will be given a specific set of instructions or training that will have spam/not-spam labels. Henceforth, you will need to evaluate and check new emails and label them accordingly. This is a simple task where you learn from the instructions. Other than this, in anomaly tasks, you will get a large group of emails without any labels, and you will be detecting unusual messages from the same. In short, learning as a process of "to gain expertise while using experience," supervised learning explains training based on learning some facts. In the spam email detection task, it is evident that you were given some data (labels) to learn, and then you were told to identify from the next task. The learner has the data in hand to evaluate and process further. This is known as supervised learning. On the other hand, the anomaly task does not involve any kind of training or learning; hence, it is known as unsupervised learning. In such cases, there are unseen instances where you are not provided with any kind of input, and you will have to predict the outcome of your skill. You will have to come with some input summary for your compressed data. Clustering is a common example of unsupervised learning. In this, clustering a data set into subsets of similar characteristics is the task. There is an intermediary system where the training examples provide more information than the use cases. In such a case, you are required to predict more information. To illustrate, you can learn a value function that describes how white's position is better than black's position on the chessboard. Also, how white pieces are dominant over black pieces. But the only information that is available to the learner is the initial positions of the chessboard with overall game positions and analysis, finally labeled by who was the champion. Such frameworks are monitored and investigated under the title of Reinforcement Learning.

There are two types of learners viz. Active learners and passive learners. They are differentiated based upon the role they play in learning paradigms.

Active Learner vs. Passive Learner

An active learner interacts with the trainer at the training sessions, by producing some queries or performing various kinds of experiments. A passive learner is the one that does not interact with the environment but only observes the data or information that is provided in training without trying to alter it in any means. One of the most common examples of passive learners is the spam filter, where it waits for the user to mark the emails with appropriate observations. To explain active learners, we can take the same example of emails where users are being asked to label the email of spam that is chosen by the learners, to understand the meaning of spam and how to label the spam emails. Another example can be of a helpful teacher in a school; the teacher usually evaluates children thinking, and based upon that, the teacher tries to make the children understand the topic. This process of the teacher that tries to feed knowledge into the learner to enhance their thinking ability and achieve their goals. In contrast, the principal of the school who observes the work performed by the teacher can be a classic example of passive learning. The concept of active and passive learners are the basic building blocks in data science. It is a branch of statistical learning. It is said that a learner is incomplete without an adversarial teacher. This statement can be justified by the example of a spam filter. If the spammer or hackers makes an attempt of spamming the filtering design, then it might lead to some complications. Not only in the case of spam filters or good scenarios but also adversarial teacher helps in worst-case scenarios. If you can learn against an adversarial teacher, you will succeed in interacting with the type of odd teacher. This was all about active and passive learners. But there is another concept of online and batch learning.

Online vs. Batch Learning Protocol

In the above comparison, we saw that there are distinct situations where the learner responds to the situations online throughout the learning process. To process a large set of data, the learner learns the setting in which he/she has to engage throughout the whole learning process, to acquire expertise only after evaluating and analyzing a set of a large set of datasets. To illustrate the same, consider an example of a stockbroker, he/she has to make some predictions about the data and update himself/herself with accurate data. After this, he/she has to make decisions based on his/her experience; he/she has collected so far. The major setback that can be observed in such a case is that he/she will gain knowledge and become expert over time, but the system might be left with minor or major mistakes. Unlike online learning, batch learning includes a batch of learners that analyses a large group of training data together. Then they might be data miners or data modelers; they jump to the output after analyzing the information.

Relation of Machine Learning with other Fields

Machine learning is not limited to specific algorithms or simplifying and analyzing various patterns; it is also connected with the fields of statistics, information theory, optimization, etc. These all are the subfields of computer science. The main goal of computer science is defined as the programming performed to the machines that will make the performance of the system more efficient and robust. Machine learning is a branch of Artificial Intelligence (AI); it helps to detect powerful patterns that turn into fruitful outcomes. In short, using Machine Learning, one can turn the experience into expertise by evaluating complex data like human intelligence. Traditionally, Machine learning was used to build automated scripts and develop meaningful patterns, but the advanced Machine learning evaluation method includes the use of strengths and abilities of a computer to behave and analyze like human intelligence.

Such tasks are very difficult to analyze manually, but thanks to advanced machine learning that eases the analysis of the system effectively. For instance, a human perception can't scan and handle a limited amount of work, it can't analyze complex data at the same time, whereas huge databases are scanned and processed by machine learning program to draw patterns that a human brain can't do. The data is generated randomly by machine learning programming. These randomly generated data are used to conclude by the learners that are suitable for the organizations. Machine learning has a close bonding with statistics and probability techniques that are proved by this. The techniques used in statistics are way too similar to Machine Learning.

We can illustrate the similarity as well as difference in the techniques used in statistics as well as machine learning by the following example: If a doctor says that there is a correlation between smoking with heart disease; you can give a statistical view like you have to view all the samples and then check whether it is true or not. This is also known as the statistical hypothesis testing method. A similar example in case machine learning works in a different manner where the doctor identifies the cause of the disease post checking the samples of the patients. In machine learning, there is a process of automation where meaningful patterns are figured out that may be missed out by human analysis.

On the other hand, in the traditional statistical approach, algorithms are the backbone of the analysis. Machine learning supersedes traditional statistical methods. Building algorithms and analyzing the information are replaced with the gathering of data and drawing meaningful patterns. Algorithms are developed for the learners to understand the computational tasks.

Another difference that can be put in light is that machine learning is well focused on finite sample bonding, unlike statistics that are more focused on asymptotic behavior. Machine learning theory works as; when you are allotted with any size of available samples, it will try to find the intensity of the samples and accuracy that a learner can predict. Not limited to this, there are various other differences between Machine learning and statistics. One best example is that while working with statistics, it is common to assume certain pre-data models i.e., Linearity of functional dependencies. However, in machine learning, you are given the freedom to work under a "distribution-free" environment. Here, the learner's assumptions are very small in proportion as compared to the learner in the statistical analysis. The learner will need to figure which model is the most suitable for the data generating process. To deal with such statistics and machine learning, the learner must be witty, and some basic knowledge is a must.

Machine learning has become a trend, and many aspiring data scientists go deep into the knowledge base of the Machine learning to understand how to develop meaningful patterns and get desired outcomes. Machine learning has supervised and unsupervised learning, but it is limited to large datasets. For every larger and complex dataset or source of information, machine learning shows some limitations. Hence, an advanced technique was developed to resolve such complex computations. This is known as deep learning, as the name suggests, every model is deeply researched in this technique. But you may wonder what makes deep learning stand out compared to Machine learning. The base of deep learning is "neural networks." Again, in machine learning, also, you may find "neural networks." But there is a huge difference between manipulating data in both the techniques. We shall see what artificial neural networks are and how they help in building model solutions and in getting accurate outcomes.

Artificial Neural Networks

Machine Learning speeds up the rapid growth of the businesses. Its role is to learn the algorithm and allow the machine to recognize meaningful patterns based upon the algorithms, develop some models and images and videos based on the learning. We learned that machine learning algorithms are built using different methods viz. Clustering, decision trees, regression methods i.e., Linear regression, cluster regression, etc. And many more. The main idea behind artificial neural networks is to recognize and analyze the patterns based on the biological models of the brain and neural networks.

In short, Artificial neural networks are a computational representation of the human neural network. It is based on human intelligence, memory, and reasoning. But why it is necessary to develop neural networks like the human brain? You may also wonder about the need for the human brain alike to develop effective ML algorithms. The reason behind this is that Artificial neural networks have proved very useful in advanced computations and hierarchical representations of the information. The basic visualization technique behind building neural networks is that passing and exchanging of the information is performed by Dendrites and axons in the neurons that connect each other to form a complex neural system. This also stores computational results.

However, the computational models must be represented in biological format to be effective.

The first-ever such algorithm was proposed six decades before to understand and build a computational model that represents a biological neural network. However, the evolution of this took a turn recently, where the version got upgraded to an advanced neural network. This version has multiple layers, neurons, and nodes. Image processing and DLP are common examples of Artificial neural networks. It has given major success in the fields of image processing, computer vision, image recognition, etc. Various applications provide very complex patterns by extracting the information from the data sets.

One of the examples is Natural Language Processing (NLP). Neural Networks prove beneficial in the event if you are working for the nonlinear hypothesis. This hypothesis includes multiple features and may have high order polynomials that might result in over fitting. Over fitting involves issues related to images and videos. They make an unusual noise rather than displaying the underlying patterns. Some examples are image recognition, image processing, etc. Neural networks are formed due to many neurons binding together to form a network. But many single bounded networks exist in machine learning. Such networks are known as "Single Neuron Network" or "Simple neural network with a single neuron."

A Simple Neural Network That has a Single Neuron

This is the simplest and smallest network having a single neuron. This neuron has a single input and one output, where it passes information of the electrical input through its input to the next network output using axons.

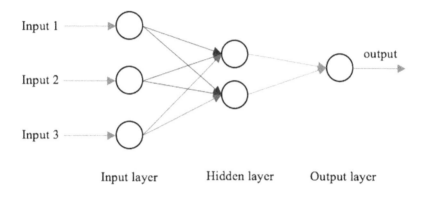

[source = https://www.researchgate.net]

Consider the above example. In the figure, you can see that a simple neuron network has a single input with one biasing input of value 1. It also has some hidden layers that not displayed on the front end. The last layer is the output layer that is connected to one of the input layers of the next network. The input layers are also known as the dendrites; in the same way, the output layer resembles the axons. The biasing input acts as constant in the network. It has a single input, hidden layer, and the output layer. To enable learning for this network, the input layers accept various featured inputs for specific training samples that, in return, feed them into the activation phase that requires computation in the hidden layer.

Neuron networks and logistic regression are closely related when you are learning machine learning. The activation function is like the logistic regression applied in the classification of the input layers. Logistic regression defines the mapping of the input-output of the neuron. Finally, the neuron network is built by a single input with the hidden layer performing computations that are finally passed to the output layer. This layer has all the required information, patterns, and data mapped. There are also multi-layered neural networks.

Multi-layered Neural Network

To understand how multi-layered neural networks, operate, refer to the below figure:

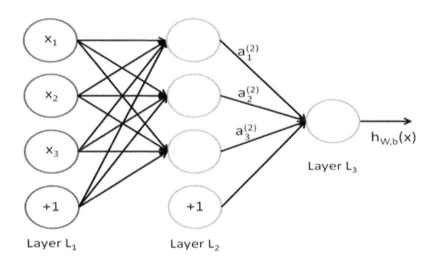

[source = http://ufldl.stanford.edu]

The multi-layered architecture has one input layer with many inputs. This is the initial layer from where the information is being transmitted to the network. It has three input layers (x1, x2, x3) and one biased input (+1). The inputs are transmitted to the hidden layer with various information for further computation. The hidden layers (a12, a22, a32) collects the information from various inputs that can form a pattern. They are known as hidden layers as they are not visible to us, but they perform the task for computation effectively. The hidden layer is known as layer 2. A multi-layered architecture contains multiple hidden layers that pass the advanced level computations to the output layer from the base level. The hidden layer units are represented by activation functions. Therefore, the main task of the network is initiated and completed in the hidden layer itself. Moreover, the network that has multiple hidden layers are used in deep learning algorithms. The basic working of the units of the hidden layer is that the first unit activates the neuron of the second layer. Activation can be explained as the value that is computed by the first layer is passed to the input of the next layer by its output by the function activation. The last layer is the output layer, where it gets the information from the hidden layer, and by default, it applies its activation function and calculates the final value of the process. This cycle completes only when the best-predicted value is given by the algorithm. This is the overall process of the multi-layered neural network.

Chapter 9

The Concept of Decision Trees in Data Science

Overview of Decision Tree

In the earlier chapters, we had an overview of Decision Trees. In this chapter, we will understand the concepts of Decision Trees and their importance in data science. When any analysis is related to multiple variables, the concept of decision trees comes into the picture.

Then you might think, "How are these decision trees generated?" They are generated by specific algorithms that use different forms to split the data into segments. Now, these segments form a group after combination and become an up-side-down decision tree that has a root node originating at the top of the tree. The main information lies in the root node. This is usually a 1-Dimensional simple display in the decision tree interface.

A decision tree will have a root node splitting into two or more decision nodes that are categorized by decision rule. Further, the decision nodes are categorized as a terminal node or leaf node.

The leaf node has the response or dependent variable as the value. Once the relationship between leaf nodes and decision nodes is established, it becomes easy to define the relationship between the inputs and the targets while building the decision tree. You can select and apply rules to the decision tree. It has the ability to search hidden values or predict new ones for specific inputs. This rule allocates observations from a dataset to a segment that depends on the value of the column in the data. These columns are referred to as inputs.

Splitting rules are responsible for generating the skeleton of the decision tree. The decision tree appears like a hierarchy. There is a root node at the top, followed by the decision nodes for the root nodes, and leaf nodes are the part of decision nodes. For a leaf node, there is a special path defined for the data to identify in which leaf it should go. Once you have defined the decision tree, it will become easier for you to generate other node values depending upon the unseen data.

History of Decision Tree

The decision Tree concept was practiced more than five decades ago; the first-ever decision tree concept was used in the invention of television broadcasting back in 1956 by Belson. From that period, the decision tree concept was widely undertaken, and various forms of Decision Trees were developed that had new and different capabilities. It was used in the field of Data Mining, Machine Learning, etc. The Decision Tree concept was refurbished with new techniques and was implemented at a larger scale.

Modeling Techniques in Decision Trees

Decision Tree concept works best with regression. These techniques are vital at selecting the inputs or generating dummy variables that represent the effects in the equations that deal with regression.

Decision Trees are used to collapse a group of categorized values into specific ranges aligned with the target variable values. This is referred to as optimal value collapsing. In this, a combination of categories with the same values of certain target values, there are minimal chances of information loss while collapsing categories together. Finally, the result will be a perfect prediction with the best classification outputs.

Why Are Decision Trees Important?

Decision trees concept are used for multiple variable analysis. Multiple variable analysis helps us to explain, identify, describe, and classify any target. For explaining multiple variable analyses, take an example of sales, the probability of sale, or the time required for a marketing campaign to respond due to the effects of the multiple input variables, dimensions, and factors. The multiple variable analysis opens doors to discovering some other relationships and explain them in multiple fashions. This analysis is crucial in terms of problem-solving as the success of any crucial input depends upon multiple factors. There are many multiple variable techniques discovered as of date, which is an attractive part of data science and Decision Trees and depends on factors like easiness, robustness, and relative power of different data and their measurement levels.

Decision Trees are always represented in incremental format. Therefore, it can be said that any set of multiple influences is a group of one-cause, one-effect relationships depicted in the recursive format of the decision tree. This implies that a decision tree is able to handle issues of human short memory in a more controlled way. It is done in the simplest manner that is easy to understand compared to complex, multiple variable techniques.

A decision tree is important because it helps in the transformation of any raw data into a highly knowledgeable version and special awareness about specific issues like business, scientific, social, and engineering. This helps you to deploy knowledge in front of a decision tree in a simple way, but in a very powerful human-understandable format, as decision trees help in discovering and maintaining a stronghold relation between input values of the data and target values in any set of observations that are used to build a dataset. If the set of input values form an association with the target value while the selection process, then all the target values are categorized separately and combined to form a bin that eventually forms the decision branch of the decision tree. This is a special case observed in this kind of grouping; the bin value and the target value. Consider an example of binning as; suppose the average of target values are stored in three bins that are created by input values, then binning will try to select every input value and establish the relationship between the input value and target value.

Finally, it is determined how the input value is linked to the target value. You will need a strong interpretation skill to know the relationship between the input value and target value. This relationship is developed when you are able to predict the value of the target in an effective way. Not only understanding the relation between input-target values but also you will understand the nature of the target. Lastly, you can predict the values depending upon such relationships.

Chapter 10

Data Mining Techniques
in Data Science

The basics of Math and Statistics help a data scientist to build, analyze, and create some complex analytics. To draw accurate insights about the data, data scientists are required to interact with the business side. Business Acumen is a necessity when it comes to analyzing data to help out the business. The results must also be in line with the expectations of the businesses. Therefore, the ability to verbally and visually communicate advanced results and observations to the business and help them easily understand. Data Mining is such a strategy used in data science that describes the process where raw data is structured in such a way where one can recognize patterns in the data via mathematical and computational algorithms. Let us an overview of five major data Mining Techniques that every data scientist must be aware of:

1. Mapreduce Technique

Data Mining applications manage vast amounts of data constantly. You must opt for a new software stack to tackle such applications. Stack software has its own file system stored that is called a distributed file system. This file system is used for retrieving parallelism from a computing cluster or clusters. This distributed file system replicates data to enforce security against media failures. Other than this stack file system, there is a higher-level programming system developed to ease the process viz. Mapreduce. Mapreduce is a form of computed implemented in various systems, including Hadoop and Google. Mapreduce implementation is a data mining technique used to tackle large-scale computations. It is easy to implement, i.e.; you have to type only three functions viz. Map and Reduce. The system will automatically control parallel execution and task collaboration.

2. Distance Measures

The main limitation of data Mining is that it is unable to track similar data/items. Consider an example where you have to track duplicate websites or web content while browsing various websites. Another example can be discovering similar images from a large database. To handle such problems, the Distance Measure technique is made available to you. Distance Measure helps to search for the nearest neighbors in a higher-dimensional space. It is very crucial to define what is a similarity. Jaccard Similarity can be one of the examples. The methods used to identify similarity and define the Distance Measure Technique

- Shingling
- Min-Hashing
- Locality Sensitive Hashing
- A K-Shingle
- Locality-Sensitive Hashing

3. Link Analysis

Link Analysis is performed when you are able to scan the spam vulnerabilities. Earlier, most of the traditional search engines failed to scan the spam vulnerabilities. However, as technology got its wings, Google was able to Introduce some techniques to overcome this problem.

Pagerank

Pagerank techniques use the method of simulation. It monitors each and every page you are surfing to scan spam vulnerability. This whole process works iteratively, meaning pages that have a higher number of users are ranked better than pages without users visiting.

The Content

The content on every page is determined by some specific phrases used in a page to link with external pages. It is a piece of cake for spammers to modify the internal page where they are administrators, but it becomes difficult for them to modify the external pages. Every page is allocated a real number via a function. The page with a higher rank becomes more important than the page that does not have a considerable page rank. There are no algorithms set for assigning ranks to pages. But for highly confidential or connected Web Graphics, they have a transition matrix based ranking. This principle is used for calculating the rank of a page.

Data Streaming

At times, it is difficult to know datasets in advance; also, the data appears in the form of a stream and gets processed before it disappears. The speed of arrival of the data is so fast that it is difficult to store it in the active storage. Here, data streaming comes into the picture. In the dataStream management system, an unlimited number of streams can be stored in a system. Each data stream produces elements at its own time. Elements have the same rate and time in a particular stream cycle. Such streams are archived into the store. By doing this, it is somewhat difficult to reply to queries already stored in the archival. But such situations are handled by specific retrieval methods. There is a working store as well as an active store that stores the summaries to reply to specific queries. There are certain data Streaming problems viz.

Sampling data in a Stream

You will select attributes to create some samples of the streams. To determine whether all the sample elements belong to the same key sample, you will have to rotate the hashing key of the incoming stream element.

Filtering Streams

To select specific tuples to fit a particular criterion, there is a separate process where the accepted tuples are carried forward, whereas others are terminated and eliminated. There is a modern technique known as Bloon Filtering that will allow you to filter out the foreign elements. The later process is that the selected elements

133

are hashed and collected into buckets to form bits. Bits have binary working, i.e., 0 and 1. Such bits are set to 1. After this, the elements are set to be tested.

Count Specific Elements in a Stream

If you require to count the unique elements that exist in a universal set, you might have to count each and every element from the initial step. Flajolet-Martin is a method that often hashes elements to integers, described as binary numbers. By using hash functions and integrating them may result in a reliable estimate.

4. Frequent Item – Set Analysis

In Frequent Item Set Analysis, we will check the market-basket model and the relationship between them. Every basket contains a set of items, whereas the market will have the data information. The total number of items is always higher than the number of items in the basket. This implies the number of items in the basket can fit in the memory. Baskets are the original and genuine files in the overall distributed system. Each basket is a set of items type. To conclude on the market-basket technique, the characterization of the data depends on this technique to discover frequent itemset. Such sets of items are responsible for revealing most of the baskets. There are many use cases available over the Internet for this technique. This technique was applied previously in some big malls, supermarkets, and chain stores. To illustrate this case, such stores keep track of each of the basket that customer brings to the checkout counter. Here, the items represent the products sold by the store, whereas baskets are a set of items found in a single basket.

Chapter 11

Data in the Cloud

ata science is a mixture of many concepts. To become a data scientist, it is important to have some programming skills. Even though you might not know all the programming concepts related to infrastructure, but having basic skills in computer science concepts is a must. You must install the two most common and most used programming languages i.e., R and Python, on your computer. With the ever-expanding advanced analytics, data science continues to spread its wings in different directions. This requires collaborative solutions like predictive analysis and recommendation systems. Collaboration solutions include research and notebook tools integrated with code source control. Data science is also related to the cloud. The information is also stored in the cloud. So, this lesson will enlighten you with some facts about the "data in the Cloud." So let us understand what cloud means and how the data is stored and how it works.

What is the Cloud?

Cloud can be described as a global server network, each having different unique functions. Understanding networks is required to study the cloud. Networks can be simple or complex clusters of information or data.

Network

As specified earlier, networks can have a simple or small group of computers connected or large groups of computers connected. The largest network can be the Internet. The small groups can be home local networks like Wi-Fi, and Local Area Network that is limited to certain computers or locality. There are shared networks such as media, web pages, app servers, data storage, and printers, and scanners. Networks have nodes, where a computer is referred to as a node. The communication between these computers is established by using protocols. Protocols are the intermediary rules set for a computer. Protocols like HTTP, TCP, and IP are used on a large scale. All the information is stored in the computer, but it becomes difficult to search for information on the computer every time. Such information is usually stored in a data Centre. Data Centre is designed in such a way that it is equipped with support security and protection for the data. Since the cost of computers and storage has decreased substantially, multiple organizations opt to make use of multiple computers that work together that one wants to scale. This differs from other scaling solutions like buying other computing devices. The intent behind this is to keep the work going continuously even if a computer fails; the other will continue the operation. There is a need to scale some cloud applications, as well. Having a broad look at some computing applications like YouTube, Netflix, and Facebook that requires some scaling. We rarely experience such applications failing, as they have set up their systems on the cloud. There is a network cluster in the cloud, where many computers are connected to the same networks and accomplish similar tasks. You can call it as a single source of information or a single computer that manages everything to improve performance, scalability, and availability.

Data Science in the Cloud

The whole process of data science takes place in the local machine, i.e., a computer or laptop provided to the data scientist. The computer or laptop has inbuilt programming languages and a few more prerequisites installed. This can include common programming languages and some algorithms. The data scientist later has to install relevant software and development packages as per his/her project. Development packages can be installed using managers such as Anaconda or similar managers. You can opt for installing them manually too. Once you install and enter into the development environment, then your first step, i.e., workflow starts where your companion is only data. It is not mandatory to carry out the task related to data science or Big data on different development machines. Check out the reasons behind this:

1. The processing time required to carry out tasks on the development environment fails due to processing power failure.

3. Presence of large data sets that cannot be contained in the development environment's system memory.

4. Deliverables must be arrayed into a production environment and incorporated as a component in a large application.

5. It is advised to use a machine that is fast and powerful.

Data scientist explores many options when they face such issues; they make use of on-premise machines or virtual machines that run on the cloud. Using virtual machines and auto-scaling clusters has various benefits, such as they can span up and discard it anytime in case it is required. Virtual machines are customized in a way that will fulfill one's computing power and storage needs. Deployment of the information in a production environment to push it in a large data pipeline may have certain challenges. These challenges are to be understood and analyzed by the data scientist. This can be understood by having a gist of software architectures and quality attributes.

Software Architecture and Quality Attributes

A cloud-based software system is developed by Software Architects. Such systems may be product or service that depends on the computing system. If you are building software, the main task includes the selection of the right programming language that is to be programmed. The purpose of the system can be questioned; hence, it needs to be considered. Developing and working with software architecture must be done by a highly skilled person. Most of the organizations have started implementing effective and reliable cloud environment using cloud computing. These cloud environments are deployed over to various servers, storage, and networking resources. This is used in abundance due to its less cost and high ROI.

The main benefit to data scientists or their teams is that they are using the big space in the cloud to explore more data and create important use cases. You can release a feature and have it tested the next second and check whether it adds value, or it is not useful to carry forward. All this immediate action is possible due to cloud computing.

Sharing Big Data in the Cloud

The role of Big Data is also vital while dealing with the cloud as it makes it easier to track and analyze insights. Once this is established, big data creates great value for users.

The traditional way was to process wired data. It became difficult for the team to share their information with this technique. The usual problems included transferring large amounts of data and collaboration of the same. This is where cloud computing started sowing its seed in the competitive world. All these problems were eliminated due to cloud computing, and gradually, teams were able to work together from different locations and overseas as well. Therefore, cloud computing is very vital in both data science as well as Big data. Most of the organizations make use of the cloud. To illustrate, a few companies that use the cloud are Swiggy, Uber, Airbnb, etc. They use cloud computing for sharing information and data.

Cloud and Big data Governance

Working with the cloud is a great experience as it reduces resource cost, time, and manual efforts. But the question arises that how organizations deal with security, compliance, governance?

Regulation of the same is a challenge for most companies. Not limited to Big data problems, but working with the cloud also has its issues related to privacy and security. Hence, it is required to develop a strong governance policy in your cloud solutions. To ensure that your cloud solutions are reliable, robust, and governable, you must keep it as an open architecture.

Need for Data Cloud Tools to Deliver High Value of Data

Demand for a data scientist in this era is increasing rapidly. They are responsible for helping big and small organizations to develop useful information from the data or data set that is provided. Large organizations carry massive data that needs to analyze continuously. As per recent reports, almost 80% of the unstructured data received by the organizations are in the form of social media, emails, i.e., Outlook, Gmail, etc., videos, images, etc. With the rapid growth of cloud computing, data scientists deal with various new workloads that come from IoT, AI, Blockchain, Analytics, etc. Pipeline. Working with all these new workloads requires a stable, efficient, and centralized platform across all teams. With all this, there is a need for managing and recording new data as well as legacy documents. Once a data scientist is given a task, and he/she has the dataset to work on, he/she must possess the right skills to analyze the ever-increasing volumes through cloud technologies. They need to convert the data into useful insights that would be responsible for uplifting the business. The data scientist has to build an algorithm and code the program. They mostly utilize 80% of their time to gathering information, creating and modifying data, cleaning if required, and organizing data. Rest 20% is utilized for analyzing the data with effective programming. This calls for the requirement of having specific cloud tools to help the data scientist to reduce their time searching for appropriate information. Organizations should make available new cloud services and cloud tools to their respective data scientists so that they can organize massive data quickly. Therefore, cloud tools are very important for a data scientist to analyze large amounts of data at a shorter period. It will save the company's time and help build strong and robust data Models.

Conclusion

This book has given you a piece of detailed information about data science. Basic data science concepts were outlined and lets you understand how to apply those while practicing data science. The practice of data science can be explained as a combination of statistical analysis, big data, and data mining.

Data scientists analyze and solve problems faced in organizations or companies involved in the business. Data science helps in connecting a firm with its target audience, improve marketing strategies, and predict future trends. Remember, data scientists are responsible for handling data right from its collection, assembly to processing, and finding meaningful insights. It doesn't end there. You need to have proper non-technical skills as well, to excel in this field. All the data that is present needs to be formatted first in a proper manner. You need to know the appropriate computations, concepts of probability, statistics, working with common databases like Structured Query Language (SQL) or Apache Hive.

So, now that you know enough about it, don't forget to become an amazing data scientist! Keep in mind all the critical points highlighted in this book and go ahead and achieve great heights in your journey of becoming a data scientist!

We hope you found this book useful, and we would appreciate it if you drop in your reviews on Amazon!

www.ingramcontent.com/pod-product-compliance
Lightning Source LLC
LaVergne TN
LVHW022321060326
832902LV00020B/3599